FAMILY TRADITIONS

Family Traditions

289 Things to Do Again and Again

CARYL WALLER KRUEGER

ABINGDON PRESS
Nashville

FAMILY TRADITIONS: 289 THINGS TO DO AGAIN AND AGAIN

Copyright © 1998 by Caryl Waller Krueger

This book is printed on recycled, acid-free, elemental-chlorine–free paper.

Library of Congress Cataloging-in-Publication Data

Krueger, Caryl Waller, 1929-
    Family traditions : 289 things to do again and again / Caryl Waller Krueger.
        p.   cm.
    Includes index.
    ISBN 0-687-08286-2 (alk. paper)
    1. Family—Folklore.   2. Family life.   3. Family festivals.
I. Title.
GT2420.K78   1998
306.85—dc21   98-24286
                                                                                      CIP

Scripture quotations are from the New Revised Standard Version Bible, copyright © 1989 by the Division of Christian Education of the National Council of the Churches of Christ in the USA.

Some of the ideas in this book are from other books by Caryl Waller Krueger. These include: *Single with Children, Six Weeks to Better Parenting, 1001 Things to Do with Your Kids, Working Parent—Happy Child, The Ten Commandments for Grandparents, 101 Ideas for the Best-Ever Christmas, 365 Ways to Love Your Child, The Family Party Book,* and *222 Terrific Tips for Two.*

The author has made every effort to make the information and suggestions in this book practical and workable, but neither she nor the publisher assumes any responsibility for successes, failures, or other results of putting these ideas into practice.

98 99 00 01 02 03 04 05 06 07 — 10 9 8 7 6 5 4 3 2 1

MANUFACTURED IN THE UNITED STATES OF AMERICA

To Lillian and Jack Waller

who through their children and grandchildren

have taught and encouraged family traditions

as gifts of love to future generations

Acknowledgments

The author appreciates the help of these friends and relatives, who shared their treasured traditions. Every idea in this book has been tested and approved with the words "Let's do that again!"

Elise and Robert Baer
Linda Bargmann
Patty Boles
Liz Daniels
Gina Froehlich
Evy Froehlich
Sheila Kinder
Connie and John King
Cameron and Diane Krueger

Carrie Krueger
Chris Krueger
Betty Lou Nordeen
Elieth Robertshaw
Nadiene Sahagun
Kent Smith
Diane Usrey
Sandy Vavra
Donna Walker

Contents

Introduction

"Oh, We Always Do That!"

Those were the enthusiastic words of five-year-old Wendy as she and a friend sat in the backseat of the car. Moments before, her dad had turned onto their street and, to the wonderment of the friend, the family had spontaneously started singing.

Wendy explained, "It's just a happy song to remind us we're near home. When I was a baby and would fall asleep in my car seat, my parents would sing it to wake me up. Now we all sing it together."

Although this coming-home ditty with the singsong words "We're almost home, we're almost home" would never make the hit parade, it was a cherished family tradition. It didn't cost a cent, yet it was a gentle reminder of the comfort occasioned by safely returning home. While singing a coming-home song is a small tradition, such small traditions are an essential part of a satisfying family life.

Today Wendy is a mom herself and sings the same silly song to her own children as they near home. In just this way, traditions move on from generation to generation. Such traditions are gifts we can give to future generations, uniting all the family in closer bonds of love.

In simple words, poet Jane Borthwick describes the importance of this unity—unity between generations, nations, religions, and ideologies:

> Let all that now divides us
> Remove and pass away,
> Like shadows of the morning
> Before the blaze of day.
> Let all that now unites us
> More sweet and lasting prove,
> A closer bond of union,
> In a blest land of love.

The intent of this book is to unite a family in love, to end divisions, and to create traditions as imperishable gifts to those who follow after us in the new century. Traditions—what wonderful gifts to give and receive!

Caryl Waller Krueger

CHAPTER 1

The ABCs of Traditions

In the past generation, some folks have wrongly labeled traditions as boring, stodgy, or out-of-touch with modern-day living. And so, many traditions have been purposely ignored or forgotten. Yet, as thoughtful folks strive to strengthen the family, they find that traditions can underlie the best parts of living: loving and being loved, benefiting from an ethical life, enjoying a happy and secure home and community.

Traditions are far more than just "nice" things to do together now and then. Traditions are the products of millions of human trials—and errors, too! The ones that last and are repeated do so because they are both joyful and useful. Indeed, they are gifts to us from the past and from us to future generations.

Doing satisfying and fun things, over and over again, lets you experience repeated events in a wonderful variety of ways—the kind of repetition that relieves the boredom that can creep into family life. That's why you want to give your family the gift of traditions.

As important as family excursions are, and as important as extracurricular activities are, there is no substitute for establishing customs that bring the family together. These are indeed "the ties that bind."

In planning your new traditions or revising your old ones, see how they connect with these useful ABCs.

Anticipation—the A in the ABCs

Youngsters of all ages gain comfort by knowing in advance that something pleasant is going to happen. Surprises definitely have their place, but nonsurprises are equally welcome. While families cannot know everything that lies ahead, there is contentment in being able to count on certain things.

For example, if it is your family tradition to serve breakfast in bed to the birthday celebrant, that person has the pleasure of looking forward to it for several days in advance. Often, the anticipation can be as much fun as the actual event.

With the anticipation factor, a youngster spends some advance time thinking about the upcoming good event. These happy thoughts cannot be underrated. They permeate the time leading up to the event, often bringing behavior that is more cheerful, gentle, and harmonious—qualities appreciated by the rest of the family.

So, anticipation is an integral part of the gift of traditions. Of course, you may give a new twist to an old tradition, but the anticipation still doubles or triples the impact of the upcoming event.

Building Memories—the B in the ABCs

When kids look back over childhood, certain things will stand out. So you want to be sure that what stands out is positive! Repeated events that become traditions can be part of those good memories. And you will have great pleasure when you see your adult children repeating some of the traditions that were part of their own growing-up years. It is sad when a family cannot look back on any activity that was so much fun it was repeated time and time again. Somehow, good memories never got built. Instead, time constraints, apathy, and valueless activities hogged the time that could have been used for building memories.

This building requires only a modest effort. A house doesn't just magically appear; it must be thoughtfully designed and then assembled, brick by brick and board by board. And once built, the house requires a little regular maintenance. The same goes for memory building—it, too, is a step-by-step process that needs to be kept up-to-date. However, memory building is much easier than house building! That's why you'll want to read chapter 2 and see just how you go about this building work.

You will find that memories in the form of traditions are gifts you can easily give!

Creative Love—the C in the ABCs

If a parent were never to speak or show love to a child, that child might truly feel that the parent did not care for him or her. But when we decide to do something special together, our inventive creativity is involved. Such caring love can take expression in a variety of interesting ways.

Perhaps your youngster enjoys curling up by the fire with a good book to read, and you add to the pleasure by serving hot chocolate and popcorn. While this is certainly not a daily event, it could be repeated weekly or monthly, making it a tradition. And the tradition could evolve into a family reading session, or a time to talk about the ideas in books. Thus, the tradition grows.

So, when you are doing something that your child especially enjoys, show your love by giving the gift of doing it again. You don't need to loudly proclaim, "This is a tradition"; rather, talk casually about it and sense how it makes her feel. Then point out that you'd be happy to do this again because of your love for her. As children grow up, you'll also find that they start creating traditions themselves. Welcome these. Talk about them. Encourage the creativity. Give compliments. Suggest a new twist. Keep them going!

15

Granted, the "s" in these ABCs is a small letter, but it is a mighty concept. According to the dictionary, stability entails being firmly in place and well-established. That's the aim of the good family nowadays. And the definition continues by saying that stable means "not easily destroyed."

When we see how many factors destroy families these days, we realize the importance of maintaining a stable family. Of course, there will be some things that fluctuate, and some things that are truly upsetting. But because of a stable base, strengthened by traditions, the family can withstand the forces that might try to destroy it. With activities that delight, events that are adventuresome, sayings that are clever, and surprises that are awesome, the family is establishing a firm, not easily destroyed foundation. Then the routine activities of family life go more smoothly and the family survives and thrives. Family traditions are like sturdy anchors for those stormy situations that occasionally occur. Thus, traditions become essential and welcome gifts for the family.

Take the Lead

It is the parents' responsibility to start the process of creating and encouraging traditions. They won't just happen by themselves. But when you see the benefits of traditions, they will naturally become an active part of your nurturing style. And soon, your youngsters will create their own traditions, too.

Keep in mind the ABCs of traditions. Give your family the pleasures of:

Anticipation
Building memories
Creative love
Stability

There is an old saying that we give our children two things: roots and wings. The gift of family traditions strengthens those roots and uplifts those wings!

"Let's do that again!"

CHAPTER 2

Yes, YOU Can Create Traditions!

Got two ears? If so, you're well on your way to creating some traditions. When you hear the magic words "That was fun!" pop out of your child, you have the first step. Your ears heard that something enjoyable was going on. So, why not plan to do it another time? Maybe it will eventually become a tradition.

But if you only had that one family tradition, it could get boring doing it again and again! However, you're saved from that fate. With the many traditions suggested in this book, you'll have a rainbow of choices for enjoyable and repeatable events. And as you read about traditions that other families have enjoyed, your creativity will be stirred into making your very own.

Thus, when you hear "That was fun!" put that activity on your Let's-do-that-again list. But remember, there are a few pitfalls in the business of creating traditions.

Don't Wear It Out

So the family liked having apples and s'mores (those gooey chocolate-bar/marshmallow graham crackers) by the fireplace? That doesn't mean they necessarily want that same menu every day of the week. Perhaps you can make it a tradition for the first Sunday of the month.

Traditions are best when they occur intentionally for special occasions. They may first spring from a random or spontaneous event. But beware of this trap: maybe the little person who said "That was fun" didn't really mean it. Perhaps it was only fun by comparison with garage cleaning or writing birthday gift thank-you notes!

You may be able to determine just why it was fun, and then, rather than doing the identical thing again, do something similar. Put your creative thinking in gear and come up with an even better idea.

Don't Make Life a Series of Traditions

Traditions are the spice of family life, not the ingredients. They add that significant special touch. But with too much spice, you can't taste the other ingredients of the day: one-on-one conversations, errands and short trips, sports events and neighborhood playtime, evening walks and an occasional pre-bed chess game. You want to avoid a day in which you always have the traditional after-school talk under a tree, followed by the traditional ice-cream cone after doing the errands, followed by the tradition of taking the gang out for dinner after Junior's team game, and followed by the tradition of chess played on the bedspread. When one tradition is heaped on another, none retains its specialness. The anticipation, the building of memories, the creativity explained in chapter 1 is lost.

18

Besides, you don't want to do everything the same way. Family life is always evolving, so work to make it evolve for the better by not making a routine of your traditions. Carefully choose your time to repeat an event: when it naturally falls into the day, when an extra boost is needed, when something special is happening.

Let traditions remain unique gifts for all the family to enjoy and share. Traditions are not amusements just for kids, they are cherished events for young and old: your family, your relatives, the neighbors, the kids on the block or at school.

Zap the Boring Stuff

Some traditions don't deserve to survive. Just because Aunt Tillie served fig preserves with every Sunday dinner is no reason you have to—unless you're crazy enough to want to.

Regularly assess those things you do and do again. Be sure they are worthwhile and worthy. Worthwhile means that the tradition is worth the time to carry it out. Worthy means that it has some intrinsic value—it makes someone happy, it comforts, or it is funny, nostalgic, educational.

But when a tradition has outlived its usefulness, gently trash it and, in its place, create a better one.

Creative Clues

In order to create and encourage traditions, you need to put yourself in your youngster's place (or your spouse's place). Consider likes and dislikes, time available, emotional needs. Ask yourself these questions:
- Did he enjoy it?
- Was it easy to do?
- Did other family members like it?
- Is it repeatable?
- Is it a springboard to something worthwhile and worthy?

At the end of the day, see if you can remember something that could become a tradition. If you come up dry (and nothing was truly fun), then it's time to take a long look at your family life and see what is lacking. You may want to read my two idea books *1001 Things to Do with Your Kids* and the sequel *1001 MORE Things to*

Do with Your Kids (Abingdon Press, Nashville). These will give you many ideas for enjoyable, even educational, activities—some of which can turn into fine traditions.

You can start by copying an idea described in this book. Do not announce, "This is a tradition." Just do it and see the response. Doing something once does not a tradition make!

Then, if the family really enjoyed it, do it again. Do not announce, "This is a tradition." Doing something twice does not a tradition make! See if you get the same favorable response.

If the family enjoyed it twice, you have a possible tradition. Wait awhile and then try it a third time. And then if everyone still enjoys it, you can say with innocent wonderment: "Why, I think this is becoming a family tradition!"

Soon you'll be thinking like a veteran tradition-maker and creating your own good ideas. As you are falling asleep each night, use those moments for creative thinking. Consider:

- What was especially enjoyable today? Did the family talk about the good and fun things?
- What events are on the calendar for tomorrow and later in the week? What can I add to make these events memorable?
- What can I specifically do to show I love my youngster?
- Is this family on a stable journey? Do we work well together as a group? Do we enjoy one another?
- What are one or two activities that we might repeat this week?

Keep a tablet on the nightstand to record your own brilliant ideas (which, by dawn, could flee away as wispy dreams if you don't write them down!). "Possible traditions" are gifts-in-the-making. Treat them with respect.

You don't usually set out to DO a tradition all by itself; traditions are usually tied to some other event: eating, celebrating, putting kids to bed, going on a hike. That's why the following chapters will give you ideas for traditions tied to specific family activities.

Now don't try them all in a short time frame! Let them simmer. Taste a few. Reject a few. Repeat a few. Tailor them to the specifics of your own family life. Get the entire family talking and participating.

But most important, start now to build traditions with your family. Don't put it off for some other day when you have more time. Right now is the time. You'll feel good about creating these gifts for the future.

"Let's do that again!"

CHAPTER 3

Mealtime Traditions

One of the easiest locations for giving the gift of traditions to your family is right at your dining table. A mealtime tradition is one that doesn't use up a great amount of time, and since the family absolutely adores your culinary talents, you have a captive audience.

For example, one family has the tradition of "Pie Day" about once a year. It may not be the most nutritious day, but it sure is fun. They eat apple pie with cream for breakfast. For lunch, they have fruit and triangular cut sandwiches served in pie pans. And for dinner, of course, it's pizza pie. Dessert is lemon custard pie.

Mealtime customs offer a variety of opportunities for subtle learning: establishing good nutrition, playing games that teach sportsmanship, appreciating family history, and exploring new ideas. In addition, traditions that teach good manners can be pleasant and even hilarious fun at times. This etiquette education emphasizes respect and dignity and can form the basis for carrying these qualities into the schools, where learning to sit still, listening to others, taking turns, and graceful eating will be reinforced.

Let's now consider the three meals of the day, plus snack time. (Traditions for holiday meals are found in chapter 9.) All these ideas have been family-tested and approved, so choose the ones that fit best at your house.

BREAKFAST

Coming-to-the-table song. One dad sings his way to the table with his rendition of "Good morning to you, good morning to you, we're all in our places, with sunshiny faces, good morning to you." It's corny, but it cheers the morning grumps.

Wonderful things are happening. Since Monday can be the gloomiest day of the week, start this custom to chase the gloom: tell family members at breakfast to watch for wonderful things that may happen during the day. Then ask them to share these at dinner. This helps to make the first day back to school and work more upbeat, and it helps kids to focus on good events rather than bad happenings.

Word of the day. Have a "Word-a-Day" calendar at the breakfast table. Make it a practice to read the word and its definition and see who can put it in a sentence. At dinnertime, see who still remembers the word and can use it correctly. This tradition is a great vocabulary builder and you'll be amazed at the words you hear popping up in the conversation days and weeks later.

24

Heavenly word of the day. Start the tradition of reading a verse from the book of Psalms in the Bible or an inspirational passage in another book. It only takes a moment and makes a great send-off for the busy day ahead.

 Hand squeezes. In the rush of breakfast, always take a moment to reach out for the hand of the person next to you. Give three squeezes for "I love you" and then be on your way for a good day. This tradition includes everyone from babes and toddlers to teens and sleepover friends.

Pancakes with a smile. At one house, Sunday morning means pancakes—with a happy look. Just before flipping them over, when the batter is almost set, use a sharp knife to make a happy face with a big grin. Another family etches a heart into each pancake. Family members have the tradition of saying "Smile, it's Sunday!"

Fancy farewells. Always say the morning good-bye in another language. Through this tradition, one family has learned eleven different ways! Try "adios," "sayonara," "au revoir," and "aloha" for starters.

Part with love. Make it a tradition to express love to each family member as you part for the day. Say it in many different ways and emphasize it with hugs, kisses, high fives, or a back pat. One family has the motto: "No going without showing that we share our care."

Bedside breakfast. When a youngster isn't feeling well (and not contagious), being in bed can be lonely. One family has the tradition of eating their cereal and toast in the sick child's bedroom. This cheery meal can raise spirits to the point that the youngster may feel well enough to join the family at the table for the next meal.

LUNCH

Lunch box messages. An "always" for one family is a message in the lunch box. It can be a newspaper clipping, a cartoon, a reminder, or a helpful or inspiring message. Some kids even share these messages with classmates (provided they aren't mushy). The midpoint of the day can be a low time for many children and a lunch box message can lift the spirit.

Pint-sized chefs. Make it a tradition that the kids work together to make Saturday lunch. This involves cooperation and creativity. Don't comment if it isn't a grand meal—just be grateful that you didn't have to make it!

Weekend artists. One family has the custom of using plain white paper place mats for a weekend lunch—especially when eating outside or when friends are over. At each place is a crayon, and eaters are welcome to doodle or make a masterpiece during the meal. And for the faster eaters, it provides a time for all-important art expression.

Five-minute warning. On weekends, when family members may be working in the garage or playing in the yard, one mom always rings a loud bell five minutes before the meal is ready. This saves giving repeated invitations, tracking down the missing, or waiting for hands to be washed. This tradition was so popular that the family mounted a big bell on a post on the patio and use it as the call to come in from play or to prepare for mealtime. They also ring it on birthdays, for winning at sports, and on holidays.

Backward eaters. One fun-loving family permits backward lunches. This means you get to eat a cookie first, then your soup and sandwich. They only do it on Sundays, and they've found it doesn't dim appetites.

DINNER

Amazing grace. Don't get stuck in a routine grace that is muttered before each meal. Rotate the saying of grace and let each person speak from the heart, expressing her gratitude for the good that has come during the day.

Five little words. Starting when kids are little, encourage the tradition of saying these five appreciative words: "Thank you for making dinner." You may occasionally hear "Thank you for making my favorite dinner," which helps you to start another tradition.

Favorite dinners. Keep a record of each family member's favorite dinner—and remember that it can change through the years! Then announce at breakfast: "We're having someone's favorite dinner tonight." Don't tell who, but let each person guess. Promise to do the same for others.

Right under your chin. Babies aren't the only ones to wear bibs! When the meal is going to be a bit messy, such as a juicy turkey burger or drippy ribs, make it a tradition that everyone—and that includes parents—tucks a napkin bib under the chin. At the end of the meal, see whose bib caught the most spills. While you wouldn't do this at a fancy restaurant—unless they give you a bib for lobster—it is quite acceptable at home.

Big Chief's chair. Create a place at the head of the table that is special in some way: an armchair, a Native American feather headdress, a fancy place mat, or an after-dinner mint. This is the Big Chief's place. While Dad or Mom may sit there for some meals, let others in the family enjoy this place of honor. Sitting in the Big Chief's chair doesn't have to be for a special occasion—it could also be for a youngster who gave a book report that day or took part in a swim competition.

Royalty Serving. Beginning with toddlers, establish the tradition of always trying new foods. Make it a very small amount at first (one pea or a teaspoon of salad) and work up to a "Royalty Serving," which is one tablespoon. Since royalty has rights, this "Royalty Serving" is all that a youngster has to have on his plate—and eat. (You can also put one tablespoon of meat, vegetable, and potato on a plate and have a youngster taste each of these before he decides how much he will eat of each of them.) This tradition takes all the pressure off because kids aren't forced to eat large quantities of something they don't as yet like, but it does point up the importance of a balanced diet. Reassure youngsters that the cook doesn't make anything gross or inedible and that one tablespoon will not harm them, but it will please the cook. You may soon find that new foods become acceptable and that a "Royalty Serving" is no longer requested.

Picky Bowl. Molly doesn't like peas, but she knows she'll be asked to eat one tablespoon of them, so let her get friendly with peas by being in charge of them. If she's old enough, she can cook them. Most any age child can season them and put them in the "Picky Bowl." Then she can proudly serve the dish to each person at the table. If you have the tradition of the "Picky Bowl" through the years, you'll find that the contents may become favorites. Occasionally reverse roles with a child who complains about food—make a face when you're served and also make negative comments on the food and the presentation of it. Kids may be shocked at your bad manners, and this example will probably cure them of the habit of criticizing food.

Traditional manners. Some social graces become so automatic that kids don't even realize they're doing them (or so we hope). These little traditions should be learned when children are young and then kept alive throughout life:

1. *Passing serving dishes.* Whether it's veggies or fudge topping, these dishes go around—never across—the table and each person takes the polite proportion depending on how many are present.
2. *Waiting to eat.* In a group of six or less, everyone should wait

until all are served. With a larger group, you may start eating when those on either side of you are served or when the host or hostess starts to eat.

3. *Salt and pepper.* As one child put it: "The salt and pepper travel together." Thus, when someone asks for the salt, they get both salt and pepper passed to them.

4. *Yucky foods.* Don't permit unappetizing comments about the food. And, if something must be removed from the mouth, show a child how to use the other hand or napkin to shield the view.

5. *Elbows and arms.* They just never belong on the table until after the meal is over.

6. *Closed mouths.* Dental work is expensive but not necessarily gorgeous to view. Teach everyone to chew with a closed mouth and not talk with a mouth full of food. Just for fun, take a hand mirror to the table and let kids see just how this looks. This experiment is usually the cure for talking while chewing.

Bad manners. A family favorite is "Bad Manners Night." It's hilarious fun to see just how many mistakes can be made (not just the good manners listed above, but also burps, interrupting, reaching across the table, and getting up without being excused). Prepare a bowl containing many pieces of paper, each listing a bad manner. Just before dinner, each person takes one (or more) and then sees if she can do the bad manner without others noticing. This tradition, which can be done two or three times a year, is a good teaching method as well as one that kids really like.

Family restaurant. One grade school boy created a tradition for summer vacation dinners at home. Once a week he'd pretend to be a waiter, complete with white shirt and order tablet. He would use the computer to print a menu showing soup, salad, main dish, dessert—whatever was being made for dinner or left over from another meal. He enjoyed taking the orders, serving the food, seating his mom (the cook), and then, sitting down and eating it. At the end, he presented an exorbitant bill (which his dad paid with Monopoly money). He continued his restaurant for many years and today he owns a fast-food franchise!

Who's coming to dinner? A once-a-year tradition can be the surprise dinner. Each family member asks a guest (a play-mate, neighbor, work associate, Scout master, and so on) to come for dinner. No one tells in advance who is coming, and the one cooking merely needs to know the total number. A big casserole and salad, plus ice-cream sundaes make a simple meal to pre-pare. With all the surprise guests, conversation will be quite live-ly. This tradition teaches kids how to be good hosts and conver-sationalists.

Toasts. Many families told me that dinnertime toasts are a tradition at their homes. One suggests that a nonalcoholic sparkling drink be used for toasting at dinner on the first day of each month when the events of the new month are discussed. (Clicking glasses of water or milk is also fine, but a special bever-age adds a little elegance to it.) Another family uses the tradition with Sunday dinner. Yet another toasts on the last day of the month when kids are complimented for their attention to chores during the month. Whenever a youngster has had a success in academics or sports, a toast can be a welcome compliment.

The complimentary dinner. One night each month, a family has a traditional dinner at which there are no complaints, no jibes, no arguing. Each person tries to outdo the others with compliments such as "This hamburger is better than filet mignon," "You look like a queen!" "You're eating so neatly that the dinosaurs under the table will starve." The statements can be both sincere and amusing. And everyone likes to be compliment-ed, even in fun.

Monopoly dinner. A family who enjoys games has a monthly dinner around the Monopoly game board. Finger foods and napkins are put at each corner and family members eat and snack for a thirty-minute game. The mom says that even the picky eaters forget their dislikes and enjoy this traditional dinner. Other games that promote family togetherness can be substituted for Monopoly.

Candlelight. Even leftovers can look great by candlelight. Have the tradition of eating by candlelight in the months when it is dark at dinnertime. Show children how to light matches and candles (and extinguish them safely). Then take turns being the chairperson of candles. One family saves money by melting all their leftover candles together and making a special candle just for dinner.

More candlelight. One family has a candle on the table for each family member. Before dinner begins, each lights his own candle and shares something that makes him happy. Although votive candles work well, the candles can also be of varied shapes and colors—a good way to use up candle stubs.

That traditional dinner with the grandparents. This can get to be a boring tradition if you don't work to make it lively. Here are some good ideas:
1. Include absolutely everyone in the table conversation.
2. Encourage a more casual meal.
3. Find alternative places to eat such as on the patio or in the motor home.
4. Let grandchildren make place cards and put them around the table to vary the seating arrangement.
5. Include youngsters in planning the menu and making part of the meal (sometimes a grandparent will have a youngster come the day before to help).
6. Use disposable plates and utensils to make cleanup easy. You can use up miscellaneous paper supplies, too, making the table look amusingly festive.

One grandparent keeps a surprise for dessert time—an announcement of where the group will go for the afternoon (park, ball game, museum, movie).

Mystery photo. A grandma has the tradition of putting a photo of a person in the center of the table each time she entertains her family. Everyone guesses who it might be and conjectures what the person did or does for a living or for fun. When dessert is near, the name of the photo person is revealed, as well as the real facts about his or her life. This kind of family "history lesson" builds memories as it educates.

Kids cook. One night a week can traditionally be the night for the older kids to cook dinner. They may serve pizza, hot dogs and soup, or a gourmet masterpiece, but the youngsters make the meal and clean up without parental interference. A favorite recipe of one family is this Seven-Can Supper. In a saucepan, put a can of drained chunk tuna and top it with these five canned ingredients (the first three drained): sliced olives, sliced water chestnuts, peas, mushroom soup, and milk (a soup can full). Can sizes are not important, but the tuna can be increased for a large family. After heating and stirring, add a can of Chinese crisp noodles.

Super supper talk. Casual comments, friendly questions, helpful answers—these are part of conversation. One family has the tradition of bringing an interesting topic to the dinner table. It can be from school, work, play, or from the newspaper. Outlawed topics are: murders, toilet training, car accidents, squashed bugs, scabby knees, and so on. Supper talk lets everyone have an opportunity to share, as well as eat.

Table reading. One family created a tradition that lasted from toddler time to college vacation years. It was to read aloud a book for ten minutes at each evening meal. The books were suitable to the ages of the youngsters and sufficiently exciting so that kids often wanted to hear more than ten minutes' worth. In the early years, the books were selected from "read aloud" lists. When college years came, the kids often brought home books to read to the family.

Background music. Since the TV is off during dinner, music can be definitely on. One family has the tradition of letting each person choose the music for a week—from a favorite radio station or recordings. However, the volume control has to be set at a level that still permits conversation! They report that it is interesting how family members learn to appreciate the musical tastes of others.

SNACKS

Snack-and-tell. When a parent is home at the time kids return from school, there is an opportunity for the tradition of reliving the highlights of the academic day while snacking together. One parent who picks up the youngsters brings granola and juice snacks along in the car. Another parent has the tradition of serving the snack on a tray in the child's room where conversation flows freely in this personal atmosphere.

Gummy treat. A surprise tradition suggested by a dentist dad is a wrapped stick of sugar-free gum as a reminder of good dental care. He pops one in a youngster's lunch box, puts it in as a placemark in a book a child is reading, or tucks it in a toy truck or in the hand of a doll or bear.

Hot cookie night. There's nothing like a hot cookie and a glass of milk before bed (or even after school). Keep on hand easy-to-use rolls of cookie dough or the newer boxes of frozen cookie dough balls. In just minutes even a kitchen klutz can come up with a very repeatable and tasty tradition.

Appetizers. So often, dinner has to wait for one family member's late arrival. One mom has an elegant solution that has become a tradition. She serves part of the meal beforehand in a location other than the dinner table. Sometimes it's crackers and cheese in the living room, another time it may be soup or a salad on the porch. It adds a unique touch and a quiet moment for conversation or watching a specially recorded program on television since the TV is off during the regular dinnertime.

Mystery Jar. Two parents who work outside the home have the tradition of connecting with their children through a container they call the "Mystery Jar." Before they leave each morning, they put a message inside the jar for after school (such as "Fruit pops in the freezer and please put the potatoes in the oven at 4:30,

375 degrees"). Occasionally a snack, such as a granola bar, will be inside the jar. Little toys, love notes, and other reminders are also easily found in the jar.

Homework break. One couple takes turns on school nights being the bearer of a snack during the homework session. Juice, cookies, crackers and cheese are brought on a tray for a five-minute break. This is also an opportunity to ask if any advice is needed (but not to do the youngster's homework) and to just keep in touch. Traditions such as these give comfort to kids who feel a bit burdened by their academics.

Fireside snack. The ever-popular Sunday night gathering by the fire has become a favorite family tradition. Popcorn and apples are served and adding a mug of soup makes it a filling meal. One family who doesn't have a fireplace gathers on the family room floor, facing the sliding doors to the backyard, where they can feel cozy while seeing the snow outside. This tradition provides a regular opportunity for the family to look ahead to the coming week as well as summarizing the past week. And, with teens, such information is a necessity! So start the tradition when kids are young and it will be natural for teens to share their upcoming plans.

Togetherness. A dad who often has to work late has the tradition of one-on-one dessert time with a different youngster each evening. The time varies, but it is always a very special fifteen minutes of togetherness.

"Let's do that again!"

Use this page to record your own mealtime traditions.

_____

_____

_____

_____

_____

_____

_____

_____

_____

_____

_____

_____

_____

_____

_____

_____

_____

CHAPTER 4

Everyday Traditions

Many "Let's Do That Again" events don't require a set time and place, they just happen naturally during the course of the day or year. These everyday traditions are ones your family can readily enjoy—they are easy-to-give gifts that will enrich otherwise routine days.

An added bonus to the enjoyment that traditions bring is that repeated pleasures add stability to life. Stability at home and in school can be the glue that holds us together—person to person, family to family, community member to community member. Such stability is one defense against family breakups, violence, and even war. When we are content with ourselves because our life is on a stable track, we are less likely to argue with others, covet their possessions, resort to violence, or refuse to cooperate or interact with others.

It is often the little things that bring us together—things that are so simple to do, but can be profound when repeated. Even traditions that help us to get organized can be enjoyable, such as this first one.

The "Morning 7s." Start the day with a tradition that I've shared with a former astronaut, a Miss America, and a rock group. If it helped them get organized, perhaps it will help your family, too. There are seven simple things we all should do each morning. The problem is that kids often do three or four of them, and then parents spend time reminding and reminding again. Copy these Morning 7s and put them on bulletin boards and mirrors where they will serve as reminders to complete these essentials before play or going out the door.

1. Go to the bathroom.
2. Wash.
3. Get dressed.
4. Tidy your room and make your bed.
5. Eat breakfast.
6. Do one of your chores, if possible.
7. Brush your teeth after breakfast.

Life would be oh so much happier if we all did our Morning 7s without argument!

Parting is sweet sorrow. When Shakespeare penned those words for Juliet to say to Romeo, he knew that separation can be truly difficult. But there's more sweet than sorrow if you adopt a traditional farewell instead of just slamming the door when you leave. One family gives "high fives." A mother uses the line: "I'm really looking forward to seeing you after school." A dad says jokingly: "Try to be good!" A son calls out: "Love you all!" And one youngster got all of his family to say the old "See you later, alligator." Find a memorable "parting shot" for your family and use it

38

often. These words are ties that bind you together even when you're apart.

"You make the rules" night. Days early in the week often need a little creative shove as the family comes off the leisurely weekend. One family invented a tradition called "You make the rules" night. Each Tuesday, children and adults take a turn being in charge. A typical night, with a grade-school-aged daughter making the rules, starts with dinner—a choice of three easy-to-prepare meals, like pasta or soup with biscuits. Next, she decides where to eat (on the deck, on a bed, by the fireplace). After dinner, she selects an activity such as a game, a walk, or a very special television show. Then, she decides whether it will be baths or showers, and if hair is to be washed. Finally, she selects the books to be read and she announces the bonus (staying up an additional five, ten, or fifteen minutes) granted for good and willing behavior. This last part helps everyone to cooperate!

Family piggy bank. "Found money" can cause arguments—a quarter on the floor of the car, a dollar bill in the wash. End the contention by establishing the custom of a family bank where all found money is kept. After two years, one family counted the fund and found over $18 in coins! So, they decided to eat lunch at a Chinese restaurant and the two children were quite impressed when the owner graciously accepted the payment in coins. Such a fund could also be used to purchase a new board game that the entire family would enjoy.

Moon music. When you see the moon, always sing the same song:

"I see the moon and the moon sees me.
God bless the moon and God bless me.
God bless the sun and the stars above.
God bless all the people that I love."

Safe jewelry. One family's tradition regarding watches, rings, and other jewelry isn't particularly fun, but it does remove the anguish that could come from losing or misplacing something precious. Their tradition is based on the line "Jewelry has only two homes: on me or in my jewelry box." If it is one of those two places, it probably won't get lost. But if it is taken off and left on a table, washstand, or somewhere in public, it could be gone forever. Safety rules should be family customs and this one makes good sense.

Shocking messages. Cheer someone's day with a short upbeat note. At a paper store, get a supply of shocking pink paper and cut it into small pieces, which are then kept at an easy-to-find place in the kitchen or family room. Use them for short messages such as "Good job on the dishes!" "Great cookie making!" "I love you," and place them on the recipient's desk or pillow. Encourage family members to write shocking pink messages whenever they have something nice to say ("Thanks for the help changing the tire" or "I love your meatloaf"). In a family with this tradition, a youngster kept all his notes on his bulletin board so he could read them again and feel good about himself.

Okays for bouquets. A high school boy noticed that there was a flower vendor on the corner of the road where he lived. All bouquets were just one dollar! So, on his way home from school every Friday, he'd buy one (using money from his allowance) and present it to his mom. Delighted to have fresh flowers for the weekend, she loved his thoughtful tradition that lasted until he went away to college. Imagine her surprise and pleasure when he returned home from college the first time and presented her with a bouquet!

Journal jottings. When a child is eight or nine years old, go together to pick out a diary—or better yet, a larger undated journal. It is for the youngster to write in, not necessarily every day, but whenever he finds something interesting or important to make note of. (The parent must promise never to read a child's journal.) Some people have continued this tradition all their lives.

Memorial Day garden. For one family it is a yearly custom to plant a vegetable garden on Memorial Day and care for it regularly thereafter. Each person chooses something to grow: carrots, beans, corn, squash, lettuce. Most kids like to eat what they grow, so add new foods each year. (In this way beets have become a family favorite.) Everyone takes part in a once-a-week weed and hoe session followed by watering the garden—and the gardeners.

Around the pool. When a mother created a pool game, she had no idea it would be continued by her children for their children thirty years later. It is simple fun to create the around-the-pool game yourself and enjoy it regularly all summer long. Plan eight in-the-water obstacles, which are made by the way you pose your body. Do them at eight different points around the edge of the pool, making kids swim through these without touching you. For example, these poses could include: standing in the shallow end away from the side of the pool but with your hands on the pool edge as swimmers go under your arms. Or, putting both hands on the coping and feet on the wall so that swimmers must pass through the "hole." Or turning your back to the wall with your hands on the coping as you arch your back to make a "hole" for swimmers to navigate. Now that you see how it works, you can create your own obstacles. Kids love to see how many of the eight they can go through without touching you.

The "Going Shelf." There's no occasion for "I forgot" if you create a shelf by the exit door of the house. On the shelf put school books and projects, lunches and lunch money, sports shoes and equipment, library books to be returned, cookies to take to Scouts, outgoing mail, ballet shoes or piano lesson books, cleaning, briefcases or other work-related items. This custom will save a lot of confusion if family members are taught to look at the shelf before leaving and take along whatever is needed. And it reinforces a youngster's desire for responsibility without nagging.

Hunts for all occasions. Go beyond Easter egg hunts by making hunts a favorite year-round tradition. Hide one hundred pennies in the sand at the beach. Hide walnuts in the backyard. Hide stuffed animals in closets and drawers around the house. Hide wrapped candy in the car to encourage a car cleanup. With a bag or basket, kids (and some adults) will love the thrill of the search.

Library corner. As soon as a little child can carry a book, establish a bookshelf for her. Show her how to care for books and how they should sit on the shelf. A family with three children has a separate shelf for each child. The youngsters are very proud of their "book traditions," which include: a special trip to the library for a card when old enough to read, keeping a list of books read, having bookplates that identify books that are lent to others, making mobiles about books, and receiving books under their pillows on Christmas night.

Parent for a day. In a family with four children, there is the tradition that one child is "parent" on the last Sunday of the month. It is this one's task to see that chores are done, arguments settled, homework completed, and special bedtimes set. They also choose an activity for the day. As the child becomes older, he also takes on wake-up calls, making a meal, selecting TV viewing, and even tucking everyone in at day's end. An interesting side effect of this "trading places" is that kids learn to become more cooperative and less contentious, since they know how it feels to be the authority figure.

Evening ramble. A dad reports on the benefits of his family's traditional evening walk. He says that walking as a group, which could include baby in a stroller, is an opportunity for family togetherness. It provides safety from dogs or unsavory people, it lets them meet neighbors as a whole family, and it's a pleasant occasion for exercise and fresh air.

Choosing chores. Wise parents will find it advantageous to let kids choose their share of the family work. At the traditional monthly family meeting the list of chores is presented and each family member selects the ones that he or she would like to do.

Kids sometimes negotiate with siblings by trading jobs or working as a team. You'll find that when a youngster selects his own tasks, there's far less complaint. And, if you let a different child choose first each month, everyone will eventually try all the jobs.

 After a sports event. Winner or loser, your child has made gains in sportsmanship, athletic skills, and camaraderie by just taking part in sports. Make it a tradition to follow the event with ice-cream cones for all the family or a hot dog gathering with buddies. One family has the practice of inviting the team to their hot tub for muscle relaxing and conversation.

Morning sing-along. A musical mom says that singing is a custom that starts the day on the right note (even though some in the family sing off-key). She starts the wake-up process with the familiar song "Good morning, good morning, you've slept the whole night through, good morning, good morning to you." Then, she encourages the singing of tunes that kids remember from children's TV shows, songs that often tie in with toothbrushing, getting along, and eating a good breakfast. Sometimes she plays rock or march music to hurry kids along as they dress. She reports that no one can be grumpy after all this morning music.

E-mail efficiency. Thank-you notes that might have been a chore for kids in the past, now become more fun with E-mail or FAX. One family has purchased an E-mail greeting card package so they can personalize their greeting cards. One mom, who writes her grown children each Sunday in order to summarize the previous week, leaped into the modern age by sending the letter by faster and cheaper E-mail. The young adults enjoy her traditional weekly letter and immediately respond with a short note about their own activities. This exchange keeps open the lines of communication within the family.

Power Plate. When a youngster has achieved something special, feels downcast, or needs a little extra love, serve him dinner on the Power Plate. While this plate can be a purchased one with the words "You are special" on it, it's fun for each family member to look for her own "Power Plate" at yard sales. That way it is one-of-a-kind. One youngster found a plate with a real gold-leaf border for just fifty cents.

Grandfather builds a house. A semi-crafty grandpa has the tradition of building a little house at each of his grandchildren's homes. At first it is just a platform about a foot off the ground—ideal for a preschooler's play. As kids get older, he attaches it to a low branch of a tree and adds a railing. Finally, he moves it further up the tree and adds a roof and a window. And, for this house, Grandma makes a rope ladder.

A ribbon for remembrance. A good custom for a young child is a special ribbon that can be tied on a lunch box handle, notebook, jacket buttonhole, or right on her wrist. The ribbon is a reminder of this comforting line: "I'll be thinking of you and loving you even while we're separated." A mother who adopted this tradition bought grosgrain ribbon in a variety of colors since her daughter wanted it to match her outfits. A son liked the ribbon tied to his bike handlebars. Another youngster preferred a bead and string reminder.

Game week. Once a year, have an entire week where a card game or box game is played for about twenty minutes after supper. Choose games suitable to kids' ages such as Uncle Wiggly, dominoes, Scrabble, Monopoly, Pictionary, checkers, chess, or hearts. The box games are togetherness fun and they help to promote good sportsmanship. A family who particularly enjoys chess keeps a game going year-round—but the opponents don't see one another at the chessboard. The game is placed on a hall table and as one of the two players passes by, he moves his piece and then puts a marker under the moved piece. (A poker chip or a fifty-cent piece works well.) Even though the players aren't together, they do talk about strategy when the game is over.

Office visit. You don't have to wait for an official "Bring your daughter to work" day in order to introduce a daughter (or son) to the place where you work. Make it a private yearly tradition. You may need to make arrangements in advance, or abide by certain safety rules if you work where there is machinery. A Saturday visit is often best. However you work it out, it's important for kids to know how a parent "puts bread on the table." And, you can probably find useful things for the youngster to do while you work. On the way to or from your work, talk about how you got the job, what your career aims are, and any special interests the youngster has regarding a vacation job or a career choice.

A teacher for dinner? While it may sound alarming at first, one family always invited their daughter's favorite teacher to dinner near the end of the school year—to avoid the appearance of "sucking up." (The teacher was one who had made a lasting impression on the daughter and helped in developing her interests and talents.) The youngster extended the invitation, including the teacher's spouse, and chose the menu for the event, which did not last more than one and a half hours. This get-together made an even more firm link between student and teacher and was a nice way to honor his or her dedication. Teachers who have taken part in such family dinners seemed to enjoy the activity—and at least they didn't have to cook after a very busy workday.

Anything goes. One family uses the custom of a weekly meeting to iron out some of the lumps in their daily life together. This session reduces the possibility of small problems growing into big ones. No subject is taboo and conversations on drinking, driving, abuse, dating, sex, drugs, politics, religion, and family relationships have been common through the years. Because these subjects were introduced slightly in advance of the age when such topics were discussed with peers, kids were eager to discuss them as a family. These meetings are one more way to keep the lines of communication open between family members, and any tradition that does that is certainly worthwhile. The next tradition ties in with this one.

Teen update. Sometimes kids don't communicate well with parents and siblings. Start the tradition of a weekly update (at

45

the family meeting or a Sunday meal), when each person shares what is going on in her life. If you begin when kids are preschool age, and keep it going, you probably won't have silent, sullen, uncommunicative teens. You'll learn about their academics, sports, and parties as well as the very serious topics of dating, drugs, and driving. Bring the calendar to the meeting so you can note each family member's events for the coming week.

Nix shyness. Children can clam up in public! Gregarious at home, they suddenly become stoically silent. One family has a regular practice that alleviates this kind of shyness. Before guests arrive at the house, or in the car on the way to a party, each family member (parents, too) tells the subject of five things he can share. These could be about school, sports, or work, or about a recent trip, the family pet, a movie, or a hobby. One six-year-old knew that having conversational topics was an important family tradition. As the family was leaving a party, he dutifully thanked the hostess and added, "It's good we're going home, 'cause I've used up my five topics."

G&G race. A fun-loving grandpa has a game he always plays when the grandchildren come to visit. Using foam or paper cups, participants decorate their own cup with markers in order to make the cup look like the grandparents or themselves. The grandfather has a large board that he elevates at one end to make an incline. Each player puts a marble under her cup at the high end of the board and holds it in place there. Then at the word "Go!" they let the cups roll down the board. The angle of the board can be changed for faster or slower racing. This competition is definitely a "Let's do that again" event. For more good ideas, you may want to read my book *The Ten Commandments for Grandparents* (Abingdon Press, Nashville).

Park picnic. Whether the weather is hot, warm, or cool, one family eats a meal at the park on a regular basis. However, rather than sitting at a picnic table, they each take up unique positions—on the platform of a slide unit, on the monkey bars, on a low tree branch, or on the end of a teeter-totter (with someone on the other end). Before settling onto the perch, each places an opened paper lunch bag on the ground below. As they eat, they toss the sandwich wrapper, paper napkin, banana peel, juice box, or other garbage into the bag (it sometimes lands nearby) so they can see who has the best aim. When finished eating, it's easy to collect the bags and errant garbage and put them in a rubbish container.

"The Wherezit Bin." Rather than rail at kids to pick up possessions scattered around the house, it's the practice in one family to have a "Wherezit Bin" in the family room where "lost and found" items are put. The bin can be a large plastic laundry basket or other suitable container. Then, when someone is looking for a missing book, shoe, key, and so forth, and wonders "Where is it?" they know to first look in the "Wherezit Bin."

Outdoor contest. When a grade school boy was asking a friend to come over and play on a summery Saturday morning, he warned the friend that there would first be an outdoor contest to weed the lawn, a contest that was a twice-yearly family tradition. It works this way. Strings are laid out to form sections—larger for adults, smaller for kids. Weeds are identified and it is made clear that pulling the roots out is essential to the pulling of a weed. With bags to hold the weeds, this family of five gets to work and after about fifteen minutes, the job is done. Special recognition—even prizes—are given for the most weeds and the biggest weed. Traditions such as these help to make work into fun.

Holiday charts. While most families have a list of chores and a chart to indicate what to do and when, one family has a very special chart for the Christmas season, starting right after Thanksgiving. For each of the two children, there is an undecorated green paper Christmas tree on the wall by the breakfast table. There is also a basket of very tiny ornaments, which are inexpensive to buy at a craft store. For each chore completed (sweep the floor, feed the cat, set the table, and so forth), the child pins an ornament on his tree. Soon they have a very festive display—and many chores willingly completed.

Cheering section. Whether a youngster is a first-string soccer goalie or sits on the bench, the prima ballerina or one of the corps, family support is essential. That's why the tradition of the entire family attending special occasions, such as recitals and sports championships, is so important. It should be a "given," unless there is a very valid reason not to attend. This goes for when Cubs become Scouts or when a youngster is a finalist in the speech contest. Knowing he has the support of family gives a youngster a greater sense of poise than he would have just performing in front of total strangers.

"Let's do that again!"

Use this space to jot down some everyday traditions for your family.

_____

_____

_____

_____

_____

_____

_____

_____

_____

_____

_____

_____

_____

_____

_____

_____

_____

_____

_____

CHAPTER 5

Bedtime Traditions

No matter what has happened during the day, bedtime is still one of the most intimate times between parent and child. It should be a time filled with love, happiness, joy, forgiveness, and hope. For these reasons, bedtime customs become a very memorable part of a family's heritage and "memory book." Don't believe that bedtime traditions are only for young children. Keep appropriate ones alive through all the years that youngsters live under your roof.

One of the most valuable components of bedtime can be mutual expressions of love. If you would like more ideas on loving your children, you may want to read my book, *365 Ways to Love Your Child* (Abingdon Press, Nashville).

The most wonderful thing. Sleep is more sweet when, at bedtime, thoughts are turned to pleasant things. There may have been disappointments during the day, but as you say goodnight to each youngster, ask him to share the most wonderful thing that happened that day. This tradition may sometimes require thinking time, and sometimes the remembrance will be immediate. Either way, it is important to acknowledge a positive happening, rather than a discouraging event. One night when a mischievous child was asked to recall something wonderful about his day, he said: "It's wonderful that you didn't get TOTALLY mad at me."

The last chance. A dad who works late often arrives home just before his kindergarten daughter's bedtime. So he has created a little tradition called "The last chance." They both like the same snack, so they sit on the kitchen table (yes, on it) each with a small glass of milk, three crackers and small slices of cheese. They feed each other (and laugh a lot) as they talk about the day.

Untraditional bath. While bath time is a very common bedtime ritual, the tradition shouldn't be merely wash/dry/get out. With two young children there can be a boat race from one end of the tub to the other, using toothpicks to push the boats along. There can be contests: how many little containers of water does it take to fill the big pail? There can be a made-up story about the ducks and frogs in the tub. Have just a small selection of bath toys and rotate them weekly, keeping them in a net bag so they can dry (and be out of the way for others using the tub). One family keeps a watering can among the toys so that the soapy scum can be washed down in preparation for the next bather.

"The PJ Evening." One family has a weekly tradition called "The PJ Evening." This means that after dinner everyone changes into nighties and pj's for the remainder of the evening. Games, snacks, book reading, homework—all activities continue as usual. Then, before the youngest goes to bed, there is a gathering on the parents' bed for a little bouncing and arm wrestling. The family advises that parents who adopt this tradition should keep a robe handy in case the doorbell rings!

My nighttime Buddy. One young boy likes to lay out his clothing for the next day—with a little help from mom. It is his custom to put the jeans on the seat of the rocker with the shoes and socks just beneath them on the floor (as if someone were sitting in the chair). Then, he places his shirt over the back of the chair with his favorite cap perched on top and his underwear hung on the arm of the chair since it will be the first to put on in the morning. He calls this clothing collection "Buddy" and he always remembers to say goodnight to "Buddy." This little tradition gives him a head start on the morning routine.

Tuck, tuck time. Snuggling under a blanket gives comfort to a young child. While saying "Tuck, tuck," a parent can go around the child, gently pushing the bedding closely around the body from chin to toes, and also around those animals and dolls who are also under the covers. One boy liked "Tuck, tuck" so much that he now does it for his own youngsters.

Magic carpet ride. Toddlers love the tradition of being whisked off to bed on a magic carpet. All you need is a small, soft rug and two parents, each holding two of the end corners. The child sits or stretches out in the middle, holding the side edges of the rug. The parents lift it just off the floor and then off to the bedroom with a stop or two along the way: to the kitchen for a drink of water, to the playroom to choose a book, to the bathroom for toothbrushing, and finally to the Land of Nod (his bed).

Bedtime tag. While this tradition is not suitable for very young children, who need a more quiet prelude to sleep, kids who are older than toddlers love bedtime tag. Played outside in good weather and indoors in bad weather, the game has rules that are much the same as regular tag. A parent is the tagger but is given a "handicap," such as having his two arms loosely tied together, or having to abide by the rule of tagging only with a foot, not a hand. When a youngster is tagged, she is the first to start getting ready for bed. You can also make the rule that it requires two tags before that child must begin the bedtime routine.

The bedtime reading tradition. Most children like to hear two or three books before bed, but don't read the same old books night after night. It's fine to end with an old favorite, but give variety to the other two or three books, which can be new books or ones borrowed from the library. Involve the child in this bedtime tradition by sitting together in her bed or a rocker, and following the pictures and asking questions such as "What do you think will happen next?" Children who have learned to read still love being read to, especially longer books called "chapter books." And teens sometimes like to read to parents. One mom who was reading to a toddler still gets teased about her having fallen asleep in the middle of a book and mumbling off into incoherence!

Surprise bedroom. One family has the tradition of occasionally sleeping in unique places in the house. Sometimes their grade school kids, as well as the parents, just trade bedrooms. Other times they let kids choose to sleep on a sofa, on the floor in a sleeping bag, in the attic, in the playhouse, or under the dining table. At breakfast the next morning they share their impressions of the surprise bedrooms and what they thought about waking up in a strange place.

Twisted endings. One family isn't content with the same old endings to familiar bedtime stories. When rereading a story to a preschool or grade school child, they have the tradition of twisting the ending into something different. The parent starts the new ending by saying: "And then an interesting thing happened . . . ," at which point the youngster lets her imagination supply a unique conclusion. For example, in the story of "The Three Bears," they decide to make popcorn instead of porridge, and eat it on the three beds.

Deadlines. Some aspects of family life have an exact time attached to them, such as the time to leave for school or arrive at team practice. Since many kids don't get adequate sleep, one of the most important deadlines is bedtime. Research shows that going to bed and getting up at approximately the same times each day greatly aids efficient functioning in morning activities such as school and work. Make it a family tradition to have a definite bedtime for each family member. This should include teens who falsely think they can survive with little sleep (although, in general, older children should have later bedtimes). Avoid the same bedtime for each child—make at least a fifteen-minute difference. Make it a "big deal" to adjust each individual bedtime each year before school starts.

Big kid's bonus. Encourage reading by giving grade schoolers a fifteen-minute bonus at bedtime for the purpose of reading, a quiet activity that makes falling asleep easier. This also shows that parents put a priority on reading. Starting this tradition with youngsters can carry over into an adult's pre-sleep reading time.

Old-fashioned bedtime. One family has the yearly custom of pretending that there is no electricity when it is time to carry out the bedtime activities. So, they resort to flashlights or carefully monitored candlelight. They turn out all the lights in the house, then see what fun it is to locate a bedtime snack, lay out clothes, take a bath, and read a story. When it's time to say goodnight they add: "Sure hope the power comes on by morning!"

Homemade stories. Not every bedtime story has to come from a book. Nurture a child's imagination by making up your own story, which can continue for several nights. Start the story yourself and create some familiar characters (a sibling, the family dog, grandpa) and also create a situation ("We've moved to the planet Mars . . . ," or "The snow was up to the rooftop that Christmas night . . ."). Mingle facts with fantasy and take turns adding to the story and giving it unique twists. You may wish to tape record these stories so that youngsters can listen to them again.

Individual prayers. When a baby becomes a toddler, he may like the custom of saying a prayer that is personalized with his own name. For example:

Now is the time for _____ (child's name) to rest,
Good and happy, by God blessed.
Angels keep watch at my side.
Safe in His love I now abide.

Make it a family tradition to make up a little bedtime prayer especially for each child.

Bedtime blessings. One family has the custom of including blessings or prayers for others when going to bed. Their blessings are sung going right up the scale. On "do" they sing: "Blessings on us all." The ascending notes of the scale can be "Bless Grandpa," "Bless Aunt Jane," and so forth, going from "do," to "re, mi, fa, sol, la, ti," and up to "do." It's fun to try and have a blessing for each note.

Grandma on tape. When visiting a grandchild, one grandmother really enjoyed the bedtime story and song session. So, when she returned home, she made a list of stories and songs she knew and just sat down and spontaneously taped them. She ended the recording with "And now across the miles, I send you many hugs and kisses." Soon the word got around to the other grandchildren and she made them tapes, too. Now, she has the tradition of doing a new one each year.

Thinking of you. When his little granddaughter had trouble falling asleep without tears, her grandpa came up with a tradition that continued with her, and was even helpful to her during her college nights when she tossed and turned. All grandpa needed to know was the approximate bedtime (8:00 P.M. for the little girl, 11:00 P.M. for the college girl). He regularly reminded her that he had made note of these times and that she should remember that he would specifically think about her at that exact time. And he did. He let fond thoughts about her play, her schoolwork, her small and large achievements, her hopes and dreams, flood his mind with gratitude for the fine girl she was. It's a fact that sleep comes peacefully when we don't rehearse problems, but rather think about pleasant events and the people who love us.

Bedtime love. No youngster is too old for bedtime hugs and kisses from both fathers and mothers. Make it an "always" that family members express love and appreciation at the end of each day. It doesn't have to be the same actions or words. Sometimes it will be a parent giving a teen a hug as the parent retires first. Or it can be a lullaby while rocking a baby, smooches with toddlers, bear hugs and kisses for older kids. Along with the physical symbol, there can be words. Sometimes it will be as simple as "Love ya!" and a good-bye wave; other times it will be a conversation concerning forgiveness about a situation or appreciation for a good deed. A wise minister has said, "Never let the night begin without recounting the blessings of the day."

"Let's do that again!"

Use this page to record your own bedtime traditions.

CHAPTER 6

Traditions for Little Excursions and Big Trips

What a thrill to enjoy a baseball game in a "traditional" ball park. Today's domed and artificial turf stadiums, the ones that are built for multisports use, just don't compare with the ivy-walled coziness of Chicago's old-but-new Wrigley Field or the much newer Camden Yards in Baltimore.

If you want a youngster to connect with the glorious past of this sport, try to visit one of the more traditional parks and talk about the old-time great players and the more genteel and gentle atmosphere that prevailed. One mother takes her children to ball games, just as her dad did with her, and she's determined to keep the tradition alive.

There is merit to some of the old ways, and what's more, such traditions are gifts to the future.

But what if you don't like baseball? There are still many excursions that can enlighten the present and open windows to the past, taking you back to your heritage. And, along the way, you can create new traditions—to bring the good of the past into the present. When you do this, you are indeed giving gifts to future generations, customs that add both fun and fiber to family life.

Snappy response. Of course you want to know that all car riders are safely strapped and snapped in. But rather than having to ask, make it a tradition for everyone to call out a selected catch-phrase when the seat belt is fastened. This also reminds anyone who has forgotten. One family chose "Snap away!" Other good lines are: "Buckled up," "Hallelujah," "I'm safe," and "Happy Snappy!"

Travel rule. One family found that they often spent more time driving to their destination than they spent enjoying their destination. So, for weekend trips, they made the "no more than one hour" rule and found that youngsters are content in the car knowing it won't be a long trip. (Longer drives were made into all-day journeys with many stops to break up the day.) Everyone appreciated having more time at the beach, the zoo, and even at the museum. So, their tradition of taking a short excursion each Saturday meant more fun and less time behind the wheel.

Singing in the car. Having a traditional start for a car trip sets the stage for happy traveling. At a music store, buy a number of copies of a simple songbook that contains patriotic, folk, and other popular songs. Start at the first song and see if you can sing your way through the book over the course of the year.

More than "once upon a time." A favorite trip for one family is the weekly library visit. They don't just borrow juvenile storybooks and adult novels. They've found a wealth of information in books about local history, sports, and hobbies. And, as the youngsters become interested in tennis or rock tumbling/polishing, they find a suitable how-to book. Sometimes they like the book so much that they eventually buy a copy at a bookstore. Another family, who also has the tradition of a weekly library trip, starts reading the books out loud on the drive home. They find that this gets the reader "into" the book and sometimes makes others want to read it, too. One family enjoys the story hours, films, and talks sponsored by their library. The dad says that it's important to check out all the many resources of the library—"a place we taxpayers essentially own."

Connecting with past history. Don't just assume that visiting a museum of history is going to be a musty, dusty excursion. One family visits their town's free historical museum before going out on a hike. This museum-visiting tradition has helped them appreciate the hill from which explorers first caught sight of the fertile valley. Another time they found that the river through their town had earlier traveled a different route and they enjoyed exploring the former riverbed marshlands. This custom of learning about one's hometown is giving their youngsters increased interest in preservation and other civic issues.

Historical markers. One traveling family imbibes history the easy way. From tour books and auto club maps, they note all the historical markers on their route. Then, when they arrive at one, they all jump out to read the plaque together. Finally, they pose for a picture at the site so that it can be better remembered. One son used the photos and information gathered at historical areas for a school project—and got a great grade!

Connecting with art. A trip to an art museum can reveal old customs as well as old costumes, demonstrating how history has evolved. One family of six has a traditional summer excursion to the art museum, where they pick out their favorite pictures, eat lunch in the museum garden, and then each sketch a modern rendition of an old painting. Starting when the kids were young, and making each trip fun and unique, they've been able to remove the abhorrence children may have for such a trip. Once, when they borrowed a book on art from the library, their six-year-old surprised them all by pointing to a picture and saying "I've already seen that one!"

Connecting with ethnicity. "When I was a child, we always ate. . . ." Most of us can come up with a favorite food from the past. Relive those good old days by visiting ethnic restaurants in old neighborhoods. Each year, one family attends a traditional Swedish smorgasbord, another enjoys a traditional Chinese New Year's feast. You may be surprised at how new foods are really enjoyed by the younger members of your family. If you serve favorites from your family's past, you'll be keeping alive your own heritage. And, if you serve traditional dishes from other cultures, you'll be broadening your knowledge of other countries.

We dig digs. A Montana family has an unusual summer tradition. They join a group of anthropologists as helpers on archaeological digs. One year they helped to unearth a real dinosaur! Although it was hot and dirty work, the education and adventure more than made up for it. One daughter said this tradition was better than going to a theme park—this was *real* prehistoric life!

Sun's up. A favorite annual excursion takes a family to a nearby hilltop to watch the sunrise. They watch the weather forecast for a clear weekend morning, then pack a breakfast and head out well before dawn. They permit kids to sleep in their clothes the night before so that they can quickly get in the car and then sleep on the way. Once there, they watch carefully for the first hint of color, and there's a snack prize for the first person who sees the crest of the sun on the horizon. Next, they have a guessing game as to how many minutes it will take for the full circle of the sun to appear. In recent years they've introduced this tradition to another family, who now join them for a yellow and orange sunrise breakfast consisting of orange slices, bagels with cream cheese, round granola cookies, and lemonade. On the way home, they see how many words they can think of that rhyme with "sun."

Similarities, differences. Once each year visit another church, perhaps one that neighbors attend. Enjoy the sermon, the traditions, the fellowship. See what is similar to or different from your own church: prayers, hymns, Bible stories, architecture, elements of the service, and those officiating. On the way home, talk about the experience and what it has in common with your church.

Fifty-cent find. A family of proud "tightwads" has the practice of visiting garage sales and flea markets several times a month. When the youngsters go along, the parents give each of them fifty cents to spend any way they wish. At home they have a show-and-tell to see the good buys: useful items for the home, toys for the playroom, sports equipment, tools for the garage—and even things to wear.

Dressy culture. Once a year, attend a truly cultural event—a play, opera, ballet, or symphony concert. (Events such as rock concerts, ice shows, and popular musicals don't really count, but can be enjoyable additions.) Plan it well in advance so when you obtain the tickets you'll get the best seats for your money. See that the date is circled on the family calendar. Cut out a newspaper review or ad and post it on the bulletin board. Get an audiotape of the music and play it during dinner several times, or in the car while doing errands. Make it a dress-up event—yes, ties and dresses are in order. It may not be as popular with the kids as the zoo, but these events are an important part of our cultural heritage, and youngsters will be happy they have been exposed at an early age so they will know what to expect later. Such events may eventually become favorites.

Lost in the country. One family's tradition probably saved a child's life. Because it was a large family and they seemed to be constantly searching for one or more youngsters at malls and picnics, they decided to wear whistles during their outings. These were just cheap whistles, but they were shrill. On a weekend hike, one child made a wrong turn and lost touch with the family. A sudden storm blew up, and the child found himself in a narrow canyon with a stream rising rapidly. He blew his whistle repeatedly and was soon located by the others, who pulled him out of knee-deep water. The whistle custom had certainly given a happy ending to a dangerous situation.

Almost home. From the introduction of this book, you will remember the tradition of singing a little song "We're almost home!" This song was used to wake up young sleeping travelers as they neared home. Through the years the song became a symbol of the comfort and safety provided by the home. Whether your home is a tiny apartment or a tri-level, it represents the bonds of family love—certainly worth singing about.

Where's home? A family who moves a lot has a unique tradition for helping the kids to get acclimated. Each Sunday, on the way home from church, everyone (but the driver) closes his eyes. The driver goes to the end of a road, or a far corner of the town or neighborhood, and then tells the others to open their eyes. At this point, they take turns giving directions in order to get back home again. (Taking a circuitous route lets them learn even more about the territory.) They now say they know their towns better than many longtime residents!

Choosing a choo-choo. One family that loves trains and train rides has a tradition that gets them on the rails even when they can't take a long train trip. In most every place they visit on vacation, there is some form of rail transportation: subway, elevated, funicular, streetcar, and so forth. They make it a point to take a short ride and also take a picture for their scrapbook, which is affectionately called "The Choo-Choo Book." On one trip, they thought they had failed to find a train to ride on, but then a youngster spied a kiddie park with a little railway. Although they felt slightly ridiculous climbing aboard the miniature train, they enjoyed the ride and even got a picture taken with the engineer.

Country rides. You don't need a destination to have a taste of country living. Every autumn a family has the custom of driving into the countryside to buy produce at farm stands and to see the colorful leaves. They have noticed the "section lines" that run straight north and south between the fields in their area (to conform to the longitudinal lines on the map for correctly surveying a farmer's property in years past). They have followed many of these straight roads until they dead-ended, usually at a quiet pond or scenic spot. They have also met some mighty nice farmers during their meandering trips.

Airport pickup. When going to the local airport to pick up a friend or relative, go thirty minutes to an hour ahead and park where you can see the incoming planes. One family who has this practice often takes a picnic lunch so that they can eat as they identify the plane types and airlines. At the appropriate time, they drive the short distance to the terminal and arrive with no last-minute rush. Formerly, going to the airport was a "duty trip," but now it is a favorite.

Eagle eyes. Kids grow up to be better drivers if they take part in this tradition. On a long drive, let one sit in the front seat as "Eagle Eyes"—the map reader and navigator, as well as the one watching for road and street signs and parking places. The tallest youngster can sit behind the driver as Engineer and watch the speedometer, other gauges, turn signals, and red street lights. Other riders can be Activities Coordinator (organizing games, songs, and stories) and Gourmet Chef (in charge of snacks distribution and cleanup). In keeping with kids' ages, trade off the jobs.

Who pays? When youngsters are able to add, start the tradition of letting a child always pay the bill at a restaurant. Her job is to check what foods are listed on the bill, refigure the bill, add the tip, and then pay it. If it is a cash payment, she should also figure ahead what the change should be. If it is a charge, she should check the charged amount against the bill before having a parent sign.

Trip sacks. One mother shares a most enjoyable tradition for their family's long car trips. Using leftover fabric, she quickly stitches a sack for each family member—yes, dad gets one, too. Depending on the person, she fills the sack with small wrapped items: puzzles, games, small toys, gum and no-melt candy, dried fruit, books, suntan lotion, small cologne, ballpoint pen, notepad, fancy sunglasses, and one larger item such as a cap or a T-shirt. She permits the opening of a gift at specific times, such as when they pass a sign announcing the name and population of a town or when they cross a state line or enter a national park. On a short trip, one item can be opened each hour. She says that preparing this tradition gives her as much fun as it does those who get to open the sacks.

Church or synagogue. One of the basic family traditions is attendance at worship services. Don't let sleeping or sports interfere (tell the coach to start an hour later if he wants your kids). Most churches have Sunday school or other activities especially for children. If yours doesn't, be prepared to occupy young children with paper and pencil, finding hymn numbers, and listening for one good idea. Create some silent hand signals to remind kids to be quiet, sit still, or to indicate that church is almost over.

One per person. Make a family tradition that in the car or at a trip destination, each person gets only one opportunity to complain. Rotate the job of "Peacemaker" (the person who must listen to complaints), but make it clear that each rider gets only one complaint. Doing this, you'll find that many problems are amicably solved without complaints at all.

Trip tradition. To get the very most out of travel, one family has a system for preparing for their trip—a system that has become a wise custom. They keep a U.S. map on the wall of the breakfast area. Colored pins show where they've already traveled and tiny flags show where relatives and friends live. When planning a trip, they use different colored pins to indicate the route. They visit the auto club or travel agency to determine route, mileage, sights along the way, and things to do at the destination. Finally, they make up an envelope for each day, showing the number of miles, the stops, the sights. In this way everyone knows what to expect, but they also make spur-of-the-moment stops and changes when a good idea turns up.

 The trip to . . . When going on a car trip longer than just a few days, buy an album or scrapbook so that the trip can be recorded on the way (since this usually doesn't get done later). Take along glue and a stapler so that maps, programs, postcards, and other memorabilia can be put in the book. Save space for photos to be added later. Using colored pens, let each youngster write comments on the pages. Keep the tradition going with each trip and then once a year, look back at one of the scrapbooks as a reminder of good times.

Graduate's choice. When a youngster graduates from grade school, high school, or college, prepare a list of three or four vacations or trips that fit the family's interests and finances. Let the graduate make the final choice. Soon, trips will be referred to as "Max's grade school graduation trip to Niagara Falls" or "Claire's college graduation trip to Epcot Center."

 Grandparents gift trip. Fun-loving grandparents have started the tradition of taking a child on a special trip when she is about to turn twelve. They offer several choices, with the understanding that it will be just the three of them. They find that the trip together strengthens bonds between the generations and provides new insights and adventures for all.

"Let's do that again!"

Use this space to record ideas for your own travel traditions.

CHAPTER 7

Traditions That Nurture the Spirit

The greatest gifts we give children are the ones that give food and drink to their thirsty spirits. This nurturing feeds them now as well as in the times when we may not be with them. Such gifts, which are often unseen but deeply felt, can be the most lasting.

Perhaps they are also the most difficult to give because they require something of us—our devotion, our understanding, our faith—handed on to them. Still, these gifts that nurture the spirit have their roots in very human experiences: conversations with our children and events that pinpoint virtues.

The following traditions help young people to recognize in themselves, and in others, their true spiritual qualities. So, in giving gifts of traditions to your family, don't fail to include some of these ideas.

Where am I going? Sometime in early January, after the hectic Christmas season is over, gather the family for the yearly tradition of making goals for the year. There should be all-family goals as well as personal goals. Family goals might be to save for a special trip, to go for a walk each day, to turn off unneeded lights, to build a patio, to read more books. Personal goals can be to learn to ride a bike, to improve a school grade, to own a cat, to eat more vegetables, to have a big party. Parents should not be judgmental about kids' goals or nag youngsters about accomplishing them. However, goals should be written down and reviewed every few months. Parents can be encouraging during this review time and even offer help in achieving a worthy goal. Attaining a goal nurtures a youngster's delight in striving for and achieving something worthwhile. This is a great way to build self-esteem.

What is our focus? If we are to nurture the spirit of our child, we must decide what is important—is it the outer or the inner person? Make it a family custom not to be impressed with outward "show." Use this example: take a small clump of mud, put it in a box, and wrap it up like a present. In a second plain box, put a small gift. Tell a child that both boxes are for her, but ask her to open the fancy box first. Note the momentary disappointment when she opens the package and finds what it contains. And then, let her open the plain box and find the little toy. Make the point that we must not let ourselves be impressed or distressed with our outer selves or the appearances of others. Such appearances can be deceiving. What really counts is what's inside us: the love, the intelligence, the sense of adventure, and the joy in living.

It's no crime. A parent should never hesitate to admit a failure. In fact, one dad has the custom of using himself as a bad example. He feels that by sharing some of his own mistakes he can say: "Don't do as I sometimes do—just do the right thing." Part of his parenting is showcasing what is right as opposed to what is borderline or wrong. He regularly reminds kids that they will just naturally grow in the ability to achieve those things that are currently difficult to do, but if they learn by their mistakes, they have not lost.

"And the greatest of these is love." The apostle Paul's words about hope, faith, and charity/love have encouraged a tradition of love in one family. From very young ages, the youngsters worked on a regular basis to earn extra money. Some of this goes in the "Love Fund." Then, when a member of the family is aware of someone in need, the money is used to buy or make items (cornbread, a flowering plant, cookies, a book, a toy) to cheer the person who is sick, lonely, or shut in.

Reach out—and touch someone. Letter writing gives new viewpoints to folks who enjoy keeping in touch. One family has the tradition of writing a letter each week, each person adding a few lines. The letters go to out-of-town relatives, friends in care facilities, or kids away at camp or school. This outreach doesn't take much time—in fact, they put the letter paper on a clipboard and pass it around the dinner table. Preschoolers too young to write add drawings. The responses to their letter writing definitely show how important it is to reach out to others. This tradition can be modified by using FAX, E-mail, or audiotapes instead of a letter.

Emphasizing the positive. The tradition of making a yearly scrapbook or photo album of family events can be expanded to bring pleasure to others. Once the book is done, it can be shared with interested neighbors, shut-ins, and relatives. For the family itself, it is encouraging to look at a single year and see all that has been accomplished. One family who has had the yearly scrapbook custom for several decades brings out the scrapbook of ten years before. By simple—and sometimes humorous—comparison, they can easily see all the good things they've accomplished in relation to the few bad events, which may seem easier to remember. This tradition helps them to emphasize all the positive events and then plan to do something similar again.

What goes around. Use a boomerang to show youngsters that what goes around, comes around. Be sure you practice first so that you can get the boomerang to return to you! Then explain that what we do eventually comes back to us, whether it's the caring act or the hateful barb. Emphasize that we can actually choose what comes back to us by what we send out. It's like the Scripture verse: "you reap whatever you sow" (Gal. 6:7). So we all need to nurture the tradition of sending out good messages and thoughts, as well as taking part in worthwhile activities and non-gossipy conversation.

A limited viewpoint. Children often make judgments based on a small, unsubstantiated viewpoint. Illustrate this by giving a child a piece of paper with a very small hole to peep through. Show how little he can see looking straight through the hole and explain that in the same way we sometimes don't see the entire picture of what is going on in others' lives. Explain that this is like our limited view about people who are judged negatively. Then make the hole much bigger and let him look through again, this time seeing more—things that were always there. Explain that this is similar to our viewpoint when we know more of the facts. Make it a family custom to be silent about someone we might harshly judge unless we can say something good.

Pocket angel. Many gift shops sell small, inexpensive angel pins. One mom makes sure that family members have an angel pinned inside the pocket of their jacket or coat. (No one else needs to know it is there unless the youngster wishes to share her family's tradition.) A daughter reports that each time she puts her hand in her pocket, she touches the angel, reminding her that she is greatly loved and cared for.

"I will pray for you." How comforting it is to know that

72

we are never alone, no matter what the problem. One family has made a practice of always responding to one another's problems with the promise, "I will pray for you." And then they do it! The youngsters and parents have talked about how to pray, and the satisfying results that come from sincere prayer.

 What's inside us? When a youngster needs encouragement to improve or excel, talk about the potential within each of us. Nurture this potential with occasions such as games and sports in which kids can improve or succeed. Explain that inside each of us is great potential—sometimes hidden but always there. Use an egg as an example. It looks quite ordinary on the outside. Yet, with proper care, an egg can become a live chicken! Likewise, we have tremendous possibilities within us that we should nourish. Make it a family custom to help each family member to work up to his full potential.

Always on Sunday. Make weekly worship services (on whatever day they fall) a "given" in your family. Start the tradition when kids are young and make youngsters aware that they are expected to attend in a good-natured way. Regular attendance will let them learn how important and useful their religion is to their daily lives. One parent puts it this way: "As long as you eat at our table for material sustenance, you will also attend church for your spiritual sustenance. Because we are responsible for you, we want the best for you."

Nurturing family history. Family ties get stronger when events of the past are relived. Start the tradition of "Nostalgia Night." You can do this with other relatives or just your own family. Several times a year spend thirty to sixty minutes looking at old photos, slides, films, or videos. Encourage humorous comments about adorable babies, hairstyles, strange clothing, goofy faces. Along with the fun will come a comforting sense of belonging to the endless thread of family history.

Family Bible. When a couple is to marry, it is a nice tradition to give them an attractive Bible—one that provides a place to record weddings, births, and other family statistics. This Bible can be made a part of the actual wedding ceremony, with the couple signing the book. Along with this tradition is the important one of also reading the book!

Child's Bible. When a youngster is learning to read, have the tradition of going together to purchase his own Bible. There are beautifully illustrated, easy-to-read Bibles that are suitable for children up to high school age. At that time, a youngster can be given a traditional version or a red-letter Bible.

Watching words. Negative words don't nurture the speaker or the listener. Make it a family custom to use positive words whenever possible. Illustrate this by putting two small glasses of orange juice on the table. Add a teaspoon of salt to one and a teaspoon of sugar to the other. Then both you and a child should take a sip of each. Explain that the sugar represents good words we say, such as: thank you, please, good, and yes. The salt represents unkind words we might say, such as: dummy, stupid, and liar. Next, ask if the salt and the sugar that were stirred into the juice can be easily taken back. In the same way, words cannot be taken back. Thus, we sometimes ruin a relationship by using the wrong words—words that we cannot take back. To continue the example, add sugar to the glass that contains the juice and salt. You will find it tastes a bit better. In a similar way, improved attitudes and actions can get rid of the negative—but it takes time and work. How much better to watch our words in the first place!

The secret place. Nurture a youngster's desire for privacy by helping him establish a secret place for keeping special possessions. However, make it clear that whatever he wants to keep to himself must be moral and legal! One family cut and framed a little door in a son's closet wall in order to make a cubbyhole for his collection of arrowheads. A dad and daughter made a small chest with lock and key where she kept letters from her grandmother. Another bought a drawer lock for the child's dresser in order to keep younger siblings out of his video games. This tradition is a symbol of trust between parent and child, but it is also indicative of the respect for certain private items, such as a journal or diary, which others cannot delve into without permission.

Loud and clear. Although youngsters can be anxious to leave church and get on with other activities, make grateful good-byes a tradition. These comments can be made to the minister or Sunday school teacher, a new friend, or the stranger sitting in the same row. Be sure to teach youngsters how to shake hands and say "Thank you" or "Good morning." This teaching of social graces can give a youngster a good feeling about himself and his place in the community.

Second sermon. Rather than waste the time spent while driving home after church, use the time for hearing the sermon (or Sunday school lesson) again. Family members are encouraged to speak as if they are teachers or ministers, giving the high points of the lessons with dignity and authority. One youngster, who really pays attention to the sermon, has even mastered some of the voice inflections and hand motions of the youth minister! This little weekend tradition reinforces what is being taught and can form the basis of a helpful discussion.

Come out and play! We know that the family who prays together stays together. But it's also true that the family who *plays* together stays together. Many families include traditional sports (touch football, volleyball, tennis, cycling) as an integral part of their daily lives. Talk with your family about sports and games that interest everyone and are age-suitable. Then learn all you can about your sport and take part in it on a regular basis. Outdoor togetherness is both physically and mentally nourishing and nurturing.

Cutting problems in half. Teach a child to make optimism, not pessimism, the tradition when confronted with a problem. With the following little experiment, show how optimism decreases the size of a problem. Put an apple on the table and call it "The Problem." Next, take a knife and cut it in half. Explain that you now have made things easier because you've cut the problem down to a manageable size. It is not magic, but a way to get rid of that half of the problem that is called *resistance*: depression over the challenge, resentment about the challenge, or apathy about the challenge. When a child sees that her attitude about a problem is actually half the problem, she can look at it more hopefully. (Now go ahead and eat the apple together.)

Hidden gifts. Although this may be difficult to accept at first, teach children that there is a gift for them hidden inside each challenge. One family has a tradition called "The Gift Box." When something sad or disappointing happens (a poor grade, the loss of a pet, an angry friend, losing the championship game), this small wrapped box with a big bow on top appears on that person's bed. The box can be empty, but you can, if you choose, put inside it the words, "What is the hidden gift?" The box is a reminder that something good will come from this challenge—that it is a way of growing spiritually and that there *is* a solution. Then, the receiver of the box brings it to the dinner table when he is ready to talk about the problem and the "gifts" hidden within it.

Annual art show. A sense of pride and a feeling of appreciation is so important to youngsters of all ages. Let a wall of the family room, kitchen, or hallway be a place to showcase your child's best work, whether it is a painting, a sports certificate, or a grade-A paper. To give these works a proper setting, buy inexpensive frames, and keep the display up-to-date. This tradition of prominently displaying good work—rather than merely sticking it on the refrigerator door and then throwing it out—nurtures self-worth and that wonderful feeling of being appreciated.

Read and rock. Researchers say that gentle rocking is soothing to the spirit. Usually babies are held and rocked, but you can continue the tradition of daily rocker time until the youngster is too heavy to join you in the same rocker. Then, let the youngster read and rock as you sit on the floor next to him. Even teens enjoy doing homework or reading in the family rocker—a marvelous piece of furniture that symbolizes home and love.

Connections. Use a piece of bread to indicate the entire family. Then tear off a few pieces to illustrate that we are part of the family, yet we are all different. What connects us are the common ingredients. You can then make the point that although each portion of the bread is unique, it was connected to the whole through those common ingredients. In the same way, we are all unique children of God, but we are still connected to God.

Patriotic present. Being proud of her country adds stability to a child's life. She belongs! She is part of something bigger than family or town. When a youngster sets out on her own—for college or a first apartment—give the unique and lasting gift of an American flag. While it is not an expensive present, it is useful, whether hung on a pole from a window or as a wall decoration. You may want to include a pole and wall bracket along with a booklet on flag protocol. One young man, who moved seven times in five years, said that displaying his flag was always a symbol to him that his true home could be wherever he happened to live.

November tradition. Show the importance of taking an active part in the political process by including youngsters in conversation about local and national legislation and elections. Do your part in supporting good government. Then instill this desire in your children. Take children, even the young ones, along to the polls with you and follow the results together on television. By sharing examples of how individuals have made a difference, you nurture the spirit of personal empowerment.

What REALLY happened? When you have no reason to believe otherwise, make it a custom to believe and respect what others in the family say. This gives confidence to a youngster's spirit, while constant challenges to her honesty cut the child down and close her into herself. Often use the phrase, "I believe you."

However, when a youngster tells something that you think is not true, yet you have no proof, ask her to repeat the story to you more slowly, asking her to tell you only what she knows is the truth. In this way she will mentally challenge her own statements and you will get much closer to what really happened.

The free spirit. Make it a tradition to revise written family rules each autumn, making them age-appropriate. Beyond these parameters, nurture a youngster's freedom to create, to choose, to experiment—as long as he is acting in an ethical and legal manner. Don't quash an idea that seems outlandish to you; rather, ask how this might be accomplished. By encouraging freedom now, while he is under your roof, he will not suddenly go overboard in unacceptable ways when he is on his own.

Touching touches. The feeling of being loved starts when a baby is born. It must be nurtured through all the years. As children grow, find varied physical ways to show love: hugs, kisses, "signing" love, back pats, lap-sitting for rocking and reading, walking hand-in-hand. Choose a traditional farewell that is comfortable for all the family, whether it is a kiss on the forehead or a friendly slap on the back.

Do it the easy way or the hard way. Explain to youngsters that many activities, such as learning math or feeding the fish, can be done the easy way or the hard way. One can put off doing homework and stumble along, or master the multiplication table and speed ahead. And, one can feed the fish each morning at breakfast, or wait until a fish is floating belly up. Using the example of making an angel food cake, a parent can explain that using an electric mixer saves both time and energy as opposed to beating the cake by hand. There are many such choices in life. Learning to make these choices nurtures a youngster's independence. Encourage thoughtful consideration of challenges and emphasize the importance of coming to parents (teachers, coaches) for good ideas when stumped. Build on this by letting youngsters know that when choosing what to do, one doesn't have to "go it alone"—one can always turn to God for guidance.

The answer is "Yes!" When you're asked questions, such as "Can I go to . . . ," "Can I change the plan to . . . ," or "Can we talk about . . . ," give a "yes" answer if possible. Show youngsters that their concerns are of importance to you. Sometimes the answer must be "Yes, but I'd like to talk about it after dinner." Or, you may say "I always like to say 'yes' but I'm not sure on this one, so can we talk more about it?" In like manner, make it your custom to regularly ask other family members, "What can I do to help?" And, when you're asked that question, suggest something that will give you and the asker an opportunity to work together. Mutual aid is a great family bond.

Being needed. Even young children like to feel that they contribute to family and community. It nurtures their own spirit when they help others. Make it a family tradition to do things that help others. This can be as simple as baking and delivering cookies, shoveling a walkway, running an errand, or reading to a vision-impaired neighbor. Customs such as these, started early in a child's life, usually carry over into adulthood.

(For more on family values and traditions, you may wish to read chapter 9 of my book *1001 MORE Things to Do with Your Kids,* Abingdon Press, Nashville.)

"Let's do that again!"

Use this page to record your own ideas on nurturing a child's spirit.

CHAPTER 8

Happy Birthday Traditions

There are very few occasions in a youngster's growing-up years that are more memorable than a birthday celebration. Christmas, a special trip, or a graduation may come close, but a birthday focuses on one child alone. No one else is in the limelight for that day.

Thus, traditional happenings can make these once-a-year days even more special. But, these traditions need depth of purpose. Certainly some are just for fun, but others heighten a sense of belonging and love. You'll note that many involve anticipation—

that all-important ingredient of traditions described more fully in chapter 1.

Happy birthday traditions carry over from the past to the present and eventually they become gifts to future generations.

These ideas can become a springboard to your own creative thinking. (You'll find many ideas for memorable birthday parties in my book *The Family Party Book,* Abingdon Press, Nashville.)

One good deed. While the birthday focuses on the celebrant, create the tradition of "one good deed," a deed done by the birthday person for someone else. A parent should remind a youngster to choose her good deed in advance of the day, but carry it out on that day. It might be as simple as taking a piece of the birthday cake over to a friend who couldn't attend the party, or donating a few of her used toys that are in good condition to a charitable facility for children. This good deed takes the selfishness out of the day and shares the joy of the occasion with others.

Wish-list trip. Go searching together, parent and child, for good gift ideas. Don't just go to a toy store, but also visit bookstores, hobby shops, record shops, and sporting goods stores. Don't buy, just have the soon-to-have-a-birthday person make a list of things (with prices) that he might like. Then, let family and relatives who ask, "What does he want for his birthday?" choose something they would enjoy giving that also fits their budget. This tradition of a wish-list results in wanted gifts, but also keeps them a surprise.

Queen for a day. Many families have the tradition of making the celebrant "queen" (or king) for the day. In fact, younger children enjoy being presented with a crown at breakfast. (It's quick and easy to make one out of cardboard and aluminum foil.) In addition, the queen's subjects can only say polite things to her, and they actually do her daily chores for her! She can also choose what she wants to eat and when she goes to bed—within reason! So, royalty has its privileges. In return, the queen must be benevolent to her subjects (parents, siblings, and friends).

Gifting the school. While the class at school may also celebrate a youngster's birthday, it is a worthy tradition for the child to give a new book to the school library in honor of the day. Checking with the librarian will result in good suggestions for books, which can be purchased at a bookstore or ordered by the librarian. Put a bookplate in the front of the book, or write on the first page: "In honor of Donald Jordan's 8th birthday" and then add the date. Classmates can be given the privilege of being first to borrow the book.

Favorite cake. Many families have the tradition of serving the celebrant's favorite cake for his birthday. Store-bought or homemade, cakes and people are matched—dad likes chocolate, daughter wants angel food, son likes banana, Aunt Sue will eat anything covered with marshmallow frosting, mom prefers a simple crumb cake. One mom, who failed to keep a record of the favorites, served angel food cake to a son for several years before he complained by saying that he REALLY likes fudge cake. But also be aware that "favorite cakes" can change through the years. Making the favorite cake adds a special "I care about you" touch to the day.

Cake for breakfast? When making the cake, also make one cupcake. (Separating out this small amount of batter won't affect the cake.) This can be served at the traditional breakfast-in-bed for the birthday person. Of course there will be cereal, toast, eggs, or other breakfast items, but the centerpiece of the breakfast tray is the cupcake with lighted candle on top. What a way to start the day!

It's a piece of cake! In one family of extremely eager cake eaters, it is the tradition that the birthday person has the legal and moral right to the last piece of cake. Others may covet it, but they can't have it. Sometimes by the time the celebrant serves it to himself, it is just a sliver, but it's his alone to eat!

One month to go. Thirty days before the birthday, accordion-fold paper and cut out a string of twenty-nine girl or guy figures holding hands. (You will need to make, and tape together, several sets to get twenty-nine.) Put simple happy faces on them (and decorate their clothing if you wish), then hang the set on a wall in the room where the family eats. Each day, the birthday child bends one head forward and down, as if the figure is watching those eating below. It gets exciting as there are fewer and fewer figures looking outward. When the big day arrives, all heads are bent back up so they can see the events of the party.

First birthday. Just because baby doesn't know anything about parties at this age, there's no reason not to celebrate. Some of your friends and relatives can enjoy cake and ice cream to mark the one-year date. Make it a tradition to plant a tree at this party with everyone helping to dig and plant. Then take a picture of baby and tree. Continue each year to take a picture of the child and the tree as both grow. Eventually the youngster may be able to actually sit in the branches of his first birthday tree.

Babies and bears. One family with a photographer dad takes a picture each month of the baby's first year. He always poses the baby with the same large teddy bear, taking the picture on the same date of the month as the birth date. This way they have a set of twelve pictures, showing how baby grew that first year.

One-on-one. A single mom suggests the tradition of a private birthday conversation between parent and child. It works effectively as the last event of the day when there are plenty of interesting things to discuss. In this intimate talk, she always shares how very important this child is to her life and how happy she is to be the mom of someone very special.

Choose your date. One family with several children born near Thanksgiving and Christmas has the custom of letting each youngster choose another date for the birthday celebration. It can be a month earlier or six months ahead—but only one party per year! For a December birthday child, a June party can be special and more relaxed without the busyness of the holiday season intruding. This also provides the opportunity for spacing out the gift-receiving, rather than having it concentrated all at one time.

Sweet sixteen, sassy sixteen. Because this birthday is very special for teenage gals and guys, make it unique. It can be the first party with grown-up touches: party dresses and suits, a frothy, nonalcoholic punch bowl, a sit-down dinner, a hired mime, or dancing with a DJ. This tradition is so special that younger children (who are not invited to the party) really anticipate their turn.

"Tell me about the day!" Children don't easily tire of stories about the day they were born. One family has the custom of mother and dad retelling the story at breakfast or dinner on the day before each birthday. In fact, they even bring out the baby book and tell who first visited, favorite gifts, and all the other memories of the first few days. And they all comment on how much better looking the celebrant is now, as opposed to his hospital photo.

Adoption celebration. Parents of children adopted from other countries are often unsure about the accurate birth date, so they may choose to celebrate on the date that the child and parent first met. One mother has a yearly party that includes other families with adopted children. At one such event, each family drew a number and in that order shared stories of their first meeting. Because some of the children were old enough to participate in the storytelling, they also shared their earliest remembrances. Food for the traditional event is always ethnic—from the children's birth countries.

Birthday ceremonies. With more and more children being adopted from overseas, adoption ceremonies are becoming popular ways to commemorate the bonds of the new family. One book, *Designing Rituals of Adoption for the Religious and Secular Community* by Mary Martin Mason (Resources for Adoptive Parents, Minneapolis), shares memorable ideas, some of which translate easily into ceremonies for birth children as well as adopted children.

Birthday circle. Find a time during the busy birthday to form a family circle, holding hands. Let each person tell something special about the celebrant and then wish him happy birthday. You may be pleasantly surprised at some of the kindly comments offered by siblings.

Grandchild gifts. One set of grandparents has the tradition of starting a college savings account when a child is born and adding to it each year. But to make the gift more memorable, they buy a college pennant each year to decorate the wall of the child's bedroom. When one granddaughter became a teen, she began to be interested in only certain schools so the grandparents obliged by buying pennants of those schools. When she went off to college, she used all the pennants as instant decor for her dorm room.

Chipper's party. Chipper loves his birthday party! He's a springer spaniel who enjoys the yearly tradition of his own celebration with the family. The youngsters plan the party with hats for all, a bandanna for Chipper, milk in toy teacups, and real birthday cake. Yes, Chipper knows how to drink from a cup! And he loves cake! Because Chipper doesn't know how to handle wrapping paper and bows, his gifts are rolled in remnant pieces of fabric, which he can more easily undo. Many of his old balls and toys are "wrapped," along with a new toy and doggie treats. As he vigorously unwraps each "gift," the family sings "Happy Birthday" to him.

After the party. When a child has had a party during the day, one family has a traditional dinner out that night. They leave the party trimmings behind and go to the restaurant chosen by the child. The family is always amazed at the interesting places the kids select for this last event of their special day. Party decor remains up for a day or so after the party as a reminder of good times.

Weekend celebration. When one family had just moved to a new city and there weren't friends to invite for a birthday party, the family celebrated by staying at an old inn on the beachfront. There they enjoyed beach walks, miniature golf, go-carts, movies, and restaurants. Now, years later, they have regular birthday parties, but in order to relive the fun of the first visit, they still return to the inn for an overnight the week of the child's birthday. In keeping with this tradition, parents and their children might pick a place close to home where they could easily return each year to enjoy part of their birthday custom.

Traditional apparel. One grandmother takes each grandchild shopping for a birthday outfit. She started the tradition with toddlers and is now buying classy clothes for teens. They always stop at the do-it-yourself photo kiosk in the mall for a picture so they will remember the day and how great they looked.

Fifth birthday. When a grandchild is five, one granddad always makes a presentation of a toolbox, containing one or two simple tools. He does this for both boys and girls. Each Christmas and birthday following, he adds to the toolbox supplies, and the tools become more sophisticated for older youngsters. For families with several children, he keeps the tools straight by painting an identifying color on the handle of each tool. With each gift, he shares instructions and a hands-on demonstration on how to use the tool. One granddaughter even took her toolbox along to college and made immediate friends with students who needed bulletin boards hung and shelves installed.

A new privilege. Meet with the birthday person to carry out the tradition of selecting a new privilege. Depending on the youngster's age, it can be getting ears pierced, obtaining a driving learner's permit (check the eligible age in your state), having a later bedtime or curfew—whatever seems acceptable in keeping with past behavior. Before meeting together, tell the celebrant to bring several suggestions in case one isn't acceptable. Make it a big deal by having the private session followed by the big announcement of the new privilege to others in the family.

Table centerpiece. One family has the tradition of stacking all the opened gifts in the center of the dining table where everyone enjoys looking at them. This is done with the understanding that when a gift has been thanked for—by phone or in writing—the gift may then be taken by the child. This tradition certainly accelerates the writing of those thank-you notes!

One rose. A heartwarming tradition was started by a pre-teen boy who each year presents his mother with one rose on his own birthday. He explained, "After all, she did all the work—I was just along for the ride!"

Treasured letter. One parent writes a letter to the birthday child on each birthday, starting with the very first. He reads them to his daughter when she is young until she can read them on her own. She has a special file where she keeps all these treasured letters. The letters cover memorable events and achievements of the past year, but most of all they reiterate the parent's deep love.

"Let's do that again!"

Use this space for your own good ideas on birthday traditions.

_____

_____

_____

_____

_____

_____

_____

_____

_____

_____

_____

_____

_____

_____

_____

_____

_____

_____

CHAPTER 9

Traditions for the Holidays

Memories are certainly built on the grand traditions of Christmas, but they are also created from the customs of lesser holidays, such as Valentine's Day. This chapter is divided into two sections: Christmas and other holidays.

Once you recognize these occasions as opportunities for memorable traditions, you'll no doubt discover you already have many of your own customs; and by reading further, you'll be able to add to them. This wealth of ideas, which connect with events and family heritage, will definitely be part of the "Let's do that again" customs of your family. And as the years pass, you will find that they are indeed gifts to the future.

CHRISTMAS

Christmas calendar. On the Sunday following Thanksgiving, make it a tradition to hang up the Christmas calendar. Use a December calendar that shows all the important dates, such as school events, decorating the house, parties and entertainments, shopping, sending greeting cards, tree trimming, carol singing, and even the date when wish lists are due.

Wish lists. Like the birthday wish lists described in chapter 8, these traditional lists are compiled at the end of November or in early December, and they should include prices. Parents can help younger children with their lists. These lists can be the result of a shopping trip to bookstores, record stores, toy stores, sporting goods stores, and hobby shops, or by reading catalogues. Family and friends who ask for gift ideas can choose from the list, still making the gift a surprise since the recipient doesn't expect to receive everything on his list. It's fun to include some gifts that are not on the list but that you know will be welcome.

Unpacking the family. Whatever you call it—a nativity, crèche, or cradle set—it can be a thrilling tradition for children to unpack and set up the stable scene. One family does it on the same date every year. They read the Christmas story from the Bible and put each piece in place as the character or animal is mentioned in the Gospels. This means that the baby Jesus will be the last piece to be reverently placed in the scene.

Christmas candle. Have the tradition of burning a special candle each night at dinner during December. While you can buy a big candle, it's more fun to make your own, but for safety reasons an adult should carefully supervise the heating part of the process. Melt all the old stubby candles you have and add some paraffin if needed. Fish out any wicks. For a new color, you can add a crayon. In a quart-size wax milk carton, affix a string to the bottom and tie the string to a pencil, which will be laid across the opened top. Pour in the slightly cooled wax and center the string. Let the candle completely cool and then peel off the carton. You can add sparkles to the outside, tie it with a bow, or place it on a bed of greens on a plate in the center of the table. Be sure to save this candle as the "starter" for next year's homemade candle.

Cutting a tree. In rural areas, and not too far from many towns and cities, you can find "tree farms," where trees are grown specifically for home use. In fact, they can be cut in such a way that a new tree will sprout from the old base. Whether you go to a tree farm or into a woods where cutting is permitted to thin the trees, it is a wonderful traditional excursion for all the family. Take a saw, a rope, and even your own sled if you're going into the wilderness. Be sure to recut the stump and place the tree in a water solution as soon as you get home. Sometimes a naturally grown tree is not perfectly shaped, but when it is decorated, it is still beautiful.

Grow your own tree. As soon as you move into a house, start the tradition of growing your own Christmas tree. Usually the property has a lot line bordering on a neighboring property. Along this line, plant a double row of fast-growing pine or fir trees that are suitable for Christmas trees. You will be surprised how quickly they grow into the perfect size for your living room. And, with a double row, the yard will still look good even with some trees missing.

Mother's Little Store. Young children often don't have the funds to buy Christmas presents. That's why one mother started the tradition called "Mother's Little Store." When shopping for family gifts, she purchases items that family members can afford in all price ranges. Then one day, a week or so before Christmas, she opens her "store" in her bedroom, where she has laid out the gifts along with paper, ribbon, and gift tags. Discounted prices are placed on each gift, prices that enable young buyers to select interesting gifts. One at a time, young shoppers come to the store (gifts for them are not displayed) and make their selections. The wrappings cost only a nickel. After paying up, each shopper returns to his own room to wrap his well-selected gifts.

The Yule log. Although you probably won't be able to follow the Old World custom of going into the forest to cut the traditional Yule log, you can still have one and the customs that go with it. Contact a lumber company and ask about getting a whole log or large split log that will fit your fireplace. Vigorously brush it off and then tie a large red ribbon around it. Select an evening for the first burning of the log and make a small ceremony as you ignite it with kindling. At the end of the evening, you can carefully extinguish the log with water from a spray bottle. You can restart and put out the log again and again. Sometimes the log has its final burning on Christmas Eve or New Year's Eve.

Christmas tree skirt. All you need is one color of fabric paint, and white or light-colored material that will go around the base of the tree to make a circular skirt. The fabric paint is put in a pie pan and each youngster presses one hand in the paint and then on the fabric. (Be prepared to quickly get little hands scrubbed clean.) A name and date is added below the handprints. Then the next year, a new set of prints is placed adjacent to the previous ones. It is interesting to see how the hands grow from year to year.

Only red and green. Early in December, one family has a custom they all love because it is slightly messy. They place old newspapers on the floor and then big pieces of poster paper. Then, using only red and green poster paint, they do fantastic swirling designs with their hands and with sponges. When the designs are dry, they are ready to be used as wrapping paper. Some are cut into 6" x 10" rectangles and then folded in half. These become the children's Christmas cards, using the unpainted side for the message. They can also be used later as their thank-you notepaper.

Just one more. While many families prefer to have Christmas morning a strictly family affair, the Christmas Eve dinner can easily be shared. One family has the tradition of inviting one special guest, who has no family nearby, to join in their celebration. Another woman started the tradition of the "Christmas Orphans." She knew that there were others in her community without family celebrations and so she invited some of the "orphans" to her home for dinner and a gift exchange. It became so popular that today her tradition includes over fifteen people, and she has learned that two other similar groups have been started.

Neighborhood cookie exchange. In one friendly neighborhood it is the tradition to trade cookies in order to have a bigger variety. Each family bakes as many kinds of cookies as they wish to trade and puts twenty-four of a kind on a paper plate and then in a sealed plastic bag. On a Saturday morning, the families gather for hot chocolate, coffee, and juice and then trade plates of cookies. Most of the cookies freeze well and can be eaten over the course of the holidays, a few at a time, or saved for a big party.

A family project. Getting those Christmas cards in the mail will be much easier if you adopt this family tradition. It is listed on the Christmas calendar as "Christmas Card Night." Everyone but the baby can take part. Those with nice handwriting can address envelopes, others can write messages in the cards and put on the return address stickers, stuff and seal envelopes, apply the stamps, and bundle the final project in easy-to-carry bags. Then all the family takes a walk to a nearby mailbox and sends them off. What a great feeling!

Card display. One family, knowing how much thought (and money) goes into sending Christmas cards, makes a display of the cards received each year. They staple a colorful sheet to the upper and lower moldings in the family room. Then, as cards arrive, they pin them everywhere on the sheet. They also started a scrapbook of their own cards from when they were married and on through the years. They enjoy looking at this series and seeing how their tastes, and their family, have changed.

Christmas tree grove. A living tree is one family's tradition. They buy it in a large container, and after the holidays they plant it in their own backyard "Christmas tree grove." Each tree has a tag showing the year it was planted. They have now covered their back property line—and as a bonus, they don't have to look at the neighbor's house anymore.

The "Gravy Grandma." One gourmet grandmother laments the fact that her grown children do not know how to make rich, lump-free gravy. Despite her many lessons, she was still asked to make the gravy for the festive dinners held at the children's homes. She didn't really mind the tradition of being called "Gravy Grandma," but she missed having her spring-type whisk for smoothing the gravy. At first she threatened to go on strike if the home didn't have that kitchen utensil! But the next year, she saw to it that one of these whisks was placed in each Christmas stocking.

Christmas dreams pillowcase. Go to sales of bedding and buy a variety of pillowcases that have a winter or Christmas theme. (You don't have to buy the matching sheets unless you want to.) Starting in December, let each family member choose a pillowcase on which to rest her head as she dreams of Christmas. Sometimes a child may wish to have her very own pillowcase, year after year. It can be decorated with her name and age. One family who had this tradition presented the pillowcase to the youngster when she established her own home.

The Christmas family. One of the most satisfying traditions is to share Christmas with a needy family. A social services agency or your church can make the connection and provide information as to ages of children and any special needs. Toys and clothes for children, small gifts for parents, food for a Christmas dinner, and even a tree and decorations are welcome. Kids especially enjoy collecting items for the family and some even use their own money to purchase gifts.

The twelve days of Christmas. This tradition can be carried out within one family or between one person and another who may not have many relatives. On each of the twelve days of Christmas a small gift is given (a pen, stickers, decorative ribbon, candy, ornament, and so forth). Within a family, the gift is secretly left on the recipient's pillow. When the gifts are for someone outside the family, the giver leaves each gift on the doorstep, rings the doorbell, and runs away.

Secret angel. This family tradition is similar to the one above. Names are put in a bag and each family member draws one. Then, during the month of December, the secret angel does secret good deeds for the other person, trying not to get caught. These deeds can be doing another's chores, making his bed, or leaving a gift. On Christmas Eve each person gets to guess who his secret angel was.

Traditional excursion. Many families have some event that they enjoy every single Christmas. Some traditions are: viewing a street parade or a regatta of lighted boats, attending a performance of *The Nutcracker* or Dickens' *A Christmas Carol,* or going to hear or sing Handel's *Messiah*. You may also enjoy driving down well-decorated streets to see the displays and get ideas for your own front lawn.

Traditional foods. Many families serve the same foods on holidays, year after year. One family has a Christmas morning coffee cake in which only one pecan is baked. The person finding the pecan has the honor of opening the first package. Another family prepares a Swedish smorgasbord on Christmas Eve so they can nibble on the leftovers the following day when they are busy with gifts. Crab and soup is another traditional Christmas Eve meal; the family covers the table with newspaper so that celebrants can tackle the crab in their own unique ways. Defying the custom of turkey or ham, one family has spaghetti every Christmas Day. Another has bread and water for lunch to remind them of the poor of the world.

The twenty-five days of Christmas. One family has a

delightful way to commemorate the month of December and to add to the family library. All through the year the parent (whose children are all under age twelve) collects books she knows her children will like. Since she will need to accumulate twenty-five books, she watches for sales and catalogue offers. These books are individually wrapped, tagged with an age range, and placed in a large basket adorned with a red and green bow. Each night, one child selects a book from the basket and it is opened and read. As this tradition increases the home library, it also increases the anticipation for the final book to be read Christmas night.

The out-of-towners. Sometimes the out-of-town sender of a gift gets no recognition in the crush of opening many gifts on Christmas morn. One family has a Christmas Eve tradition that gives special recognition to out-of-towners and their gifts. After dinner, these gifts are opened, and then the givers are telephoned. In this way, youngsters very clearly identify the gift with the giver.

Not on key. The members of one family, who admit they don't sing too well, have a tradition that they have continued for decades. It starts with cookie baking in the weeks before Christmas. Then, after their big Christmas Eve dinner, they make up small plates of cookies and candy and tie them with festive bows. Since all feel the need for a good walk, young and old set out together to make stops around the neighborhood, presenting their cookie gifts and singing one easy carol: "We wish you a Merry Christmas and a Happy New Year."

Christmas Eve party for Jesus. Since the birth of Jesus is what is being celebrated, one family has a party in his honor, complete with a birthday cake. Then they act out the story with family members assigned to be Mary, Joseph, angels, kings, Herod, shepherds and sheep, and the baby. While some play several roles, the father always volunteers to be the donkey and hopes for a lightweight Mary to ride on his back! In Jesus' honor, they always present a gift to a charitable institution.

Stealing gifts. When an office group gets together for their yearly party, they find it fun to play "Stealing Gifts." Each person brings a wrapped gift (set a limit, such as $15). Each person picks a number out of a bag, which indicates the order of choosing a gift. Number 1 goes first, then number 2, each opening their gift and showing it to the group. At this point, number 2 may "steal" number 1's gift, giving his in return. And so the opening of gifts continues, as well as the stealing of any of the preceding gifts. However, a gift can only be stolen three times and then it must stay put. At the very end, number 1 gets the chance to make the final steal.

Christmas stars. As the last experience on Christmas Eve, go outside and look up at the stars. These are the same heavens that the shepherds saw. Bundle up and just quietly watch the sky before getting ready for bed. You may even want to say your bedtime prayers out there.

Christmas Eve pj's. Who wants to look tacky for Christmas morning? Start the tradition of giving new pajamas and nighties to the kids on Christmas Eve. It is an exciting "first gift" before a good night's sleep and waking up for gift opening and photo time. One family chooses a different fabric each year for the homemade matching outfits. Another family even includes new sleep attire for the parents.

The Christmas Eve story. Even after children have long given up belief in Santa, continue the tradition of reading aloud Clement Moore's "A Visit from Saint Nicholas," which begins: " 'Twas the night before Christmas. . . ." Children will love to repeat the lines along with you, right up to the end line: "And to all, a good night!"

Christmas breakfast. When excitement takes over, breakfast might be brushed aside on Christmas morning. One family has an answer—the tradition of opening gifts one at a time, allowing for investigating the gift and also appreciating it. So, while one person is opening and admiring a gift, the others can be break-fasting. This is done by preparing some things the night before and a few others that morning, then placing everything on the coffee table in the midst of the family circle. Tasty breakfast items include blueberry muffins (made earlier and reheated), sausage links on toothpicks, cheese and crackers, salsa and chips, toasted bagel chips, deviled eggs (made the day before), slices of pears and apples, coffee cake (made earlier in the month, frozen, thawed, and heated), Christmas cookies and candies, juice and coffee. The variety of food means that even the picky eaters will find something they like. And the large amount of food should be sufficient so that no other food is required until Christmas dinner.

Before unwrapping. To set the tone for Christmas morning, one family takes turns reading the Christmas story as told in the Gospels of the Bible. Another family made a booklet of it, complete with illustrations drawn by the children. The citations they chose are:

Micah 5:2
Isaiah 40:1-5, and 9:2, 6-7
Matthew 1:18-23
Luke 2:1, 3-7, 8-18, 20
Matthew 2:1-12
Luke 2:40
Matthew 4:23-24; 5:2, 16; and 10:8
John 13:34; 21:25
Revelation 19:6, 16

Christmas stockings. For many families who keep the Santa tradition as a happy myth, Christmas gifts placed by Santa in stockings are still a highlight. Little gifts, wrapped or unwrapped, useful or funny, are stuffed inside the stockings. One family also has the tradition of including notepaper in each stocking as a reminder to write thank-you notes. There is no formality about opening stocking gifts, but everyone gets to share a few of the unique items after the excitement of opening everything.

Christmas morning hats. One family has a red and white cap for each family member—even one for the baby. This tradition makes their yearly Christmas morning photos look quite festive.

 Who gave the gifts? One family has the custom of giving the gifts they have purchased on behalf of very special people. Of course there will be gifts from parents and siblings, but the parents also sign gift cards from the Christmas Angel, Baby Jesus, and Rudolph the red-nosed reindeer. And, there is also a big bag of gifts marked from Santa—even though no one believes in Santa anymore. But they say they do believe in Santa as the spirit of Christmas love. Tags on gifts are always read loudly and clearly.

 Great-grandma's gifts. One clever woman collected interesting gifts for the family all through the year. She wrapped them and put a long string on each one and placed them in a big bag with the strings hanging out. Then, each person took a turn pulling on a string and finding a gift attached to it. After all had unwrapped their goodies, they were welcome to exchange them with one another. It was memorable fun!

 Holding hands. When the family is scattered at Christmas, it's time to establish traditions just for two. One couple finds that they spend the holiday alone with each other about every other year, but they make it special. In the morning they take a snowy walk together and make a snowman on the front lawn. In the afternoon they chat with faraway children and grandchildren and hear about their festivities. In the late afternoon they dress up for a very special dinner. The husband makes his famous shrimp cocktail and she makes a mushroom-stuffed chicken dish as he sets the table by the fireplace. Then they eat by candlelight and firelight. Finally, they exchange gifts and then sit by the fire reliving the wonderful Christmases they've had together. It is peaceful as well as romantic.

 Phone calls. The holiday season can be a lonely time for those living by themselves. One family has a list of relatives and friends who enjoy a telephone chat. They keep the list from year to year and usually telephone on Christmas night when everyone has something to share.

One final gift. When the house is filled with wonderful gifts and rumpled wrapping paper, it's a nice tradition to save one small gift for dinner on Christmas Day. One family calls these "table gifts" because they are small items that are put at each place on the table. Over the years they have had table gifts of little toys, magic tricks, key rings, wallets, and jewelry.

One more final gift. Since the time when the children were little, one couple always put a book under each child's pillow on Christmas Day night. The parents did the same for each other. And, at breakfast the next day, they shared what they received. Although those children are now grown, the tradition continues when the young adults spend the night and often place books under the parents' pillows.

Under the tree. Although the gifts are gone from under the tree, start the tradition of a week-after-Christmas pajama party in the living room. With sleeping bags, let everyone settle in under the tree and look up through the branches, dreaming of Christmases to come. Parents should turn off the tree lights when kids are asleep—and then they, too, can sleep under the tree or on a nearby couch.

Two Christmases. Since this holiday is so beloved, why not celebrate it twice each year? One family does just that with a second Christmas held in July. A few weeks before, they exchange names and each person buys just one gift. Then, on the chosen date they bring out one or two favorite decorations. The dinner includes turkey and all the trimmings, and after the big meal the gifts are exchanged. Then they go out in the backyard and sing a few Christmas carols—much to the amusement of the neighbors!

VALENTINE'S DAY

No mush. Sometimes kids feel that Valentine's Day is too sentimental. They have trouble verbalizing their love for family members, especially siblings. Help them to express love and appreciation through this tradition that one family has had for about twelve years. They put Valentines they have made and written under one another's pillows. That way no one else gets to read them. And by writing one to each child, parents make sure that each person gets at least one love note.

Clues to candy. A sentimental man takes his three children to a popular candy store each year to buy a small heart-shaped box of candy for his sweetheart—their mom. Each child chooses two pieces of candy to fill the candy heart. At home, the heart is secretly hidden in the house. After supper on Valentine's Day, the mom is given clues: Go to where things come clean (the washer), find where the Simpsons live (TV set), travel to the arctic region (the freezer). She follows the clues to the candy box. And when she eats a piece of candy, she tries to guess who chose that particular one.

EASTER

Name those eggs. When family members are coloring and decorating eggs, be sure they include on the underside of the egg the signature of the artist as well as the name of the person for whom it is made. You can keep these decorated eggs for decades if you blow them out (put a small hole in each end and blow hard) and use the contents for scrambled eggs. Salvage egg cartons as safe places to keep the eggs for following years. Display them all on fake grass in the center of the dining table and see how the art improves each year.

The day after Easter. The decorating of eggs is very popular in Hungary. This tradition is based on a less-known Hungarian custom. On the day after Easter, each family fills a basket with decorated eggs and goes visiting, leaving an egg at each stop. Since the eggs have been blown out, they last indefinitely and the gifted eggs are added to each family's display of eggs in the center of their dining table.

APRIL FOOL'S DAY

Oh, those pranks! Pranks that do no harm enliven this day of fun. You can increase your repertoire of pranks by exchanging ideas with friends. Some include: hiding an alarm clock in a drawer, short-sheeting beds, placing a cup of water on top of an open door, setting the table UNDER the table, using safe food coloring in foods and beverages, placing plastic insects in water glasses and wash bowls, and rubber-banding the kitchen sink sprayer so that it is automatically on when the water is turned on! (This one's a real winner.) Get the entire family into the act of having harmless fun. It's a good exercise on how to graciously give and receive pranks.

MOTHER'S DAY

Mom's week. Rather than a one-day celebration, have the tradition of an entire week honoring mom. Dad or another adult can help the youngsters make a booklet out of seven envelopes, which are stapled together and labeled for each day of the week. Inside each envelope is a promised good deed or event such as: making lunch, reading poetry to her, watching a sibling so she can have a long bubble bath, going to a movie, and so forth. The last envelope always contains a love letter to mother.

A garden of love. One family, who enjoys their backyard, plants a garden in mom's honor each May. Everyone but mom does the work—she gets to sit on the patio and supervise. The family doesn't tell her what seeds they've bought, but the garden always includes her favorites.

FATHER'S DAY

Surprise! While mother may have had breakfast in bed, a nice tradition for a dad is a surprise party with another family. One year it was at the beach with gifts of new beach chairs and matching T-shirts. Another year it was a tailgate supper at the ballpark and tickets to the game. And one year, the kids made a plan to stay overnight with nearby relatives and gave their parents the opportunity for an adults-only party for dinner and a play.

New dad. When one couple had their first baby, the wife made all the plans for her husband's first Father's Day. She pretended that she wanted him to go along on an errand, and with baby in the car seat and a lavish supper hidden in the trunk, they set out for a nearby park at a lake. A candlelight picnic followed and they were home in time to put baby in his bed and enjoy a newly released video the mom had picked out. (This was a movie they had wanted to see but didn't because of the new baby.) It was so successful that they repeat the custom yearly as their little family grows.

INDEPENDENCE DAY

Fearsome firecrackers. When a young child is frightened by the sound of fireworks, start the tradition of everyone shouting "Happy 4th of July!" when they hear a firecracker go off. This removes the tension and kids look forward to the next blast and the opportunity to shout. A few weeks after one family did this, their toddler heard a car backfire and shouted "Happy 4th of July!" This tradition is carried further in one family: When they are out driving and see a pumpkin in late autumn, they shout "Happy Thanksgiving!" When they see outdoor Christmas decoration lights, they call out "Merry Christmas!"

Ice-cream social. As in the good old days, ice cream and the 4th of July just go together. One neighborhood has a party every year. First, the kids make a parade of decorated pets, bicycles, and strollers—each getting a small prize. Then the party moves to a big backyard where the chairperson of the event introduces those who've moved in since the previous party, and all have an opportunity to chat while the kids play. Finally, there is a table with many varieties of ice cream and toppings, which cause some participants to try to out-do one another with fabulous concoctions.

FALL FESTIVAL

A pumpkin's life. When the family goes out to pick pumpkins, start the tradition of giving a name and identity to each one. After all, these pumpkins are going to be an integral part of activities at the end of October. (Some names are Peter Pumpkin, Sally Squash, and Jack O. Lantern.) Also, choose one that is an impossible shape and name it Dumbo. When cutting pumpkins, be sure to save all the seeds, which become great munchies when roasted. Of course, you will carve pumpkins and probably keep them on the doorstep until they get moldy. But refrigerate Dumbo and use him for the special purpose of providing good things to eat, such as pumpkin pie and pumpkin bread. Freeze some pumpkin muffins, which you can have for breakfast on Thanksgiving morning.

The Great Pumpkin. Overloaded with candy? While some families put the candy in the freezer for later snacking, you can put a permanent blitz on sugar consumption this easy way. One family has invented the tradition of the "Great Pumpkin" (an orange version of the tooth fairy). You will need to buy a large plastic pumpkin. When kids return from trick-or-treating with an overflowing bag of candy, tell them that the Great Pumpkin has a gift for children who give him candy—more candy turns into a better gift. The children look over their collection of candy and usually put almost all of it in the pumpkin, keeping just a few prime pieces for munching that day and the next. After they fall asleep, the pumpkin is taken away. In its place is a wrapped gift for each child. Although one child is old enough to know that the Great Pumpkin is just a happy myth, she still likes the trade of candy for gifts and the good feeling of giving extra candy to those who got none.

THANKSGIVING

The grateful chain. Starting early in November, many families have the tradition of making links for a chain that expresses their gratitude. Each night at dinner, using red and green strips of paper, they write something for which they are grateful. These are made into links and the chain is started. Eventually, it is long enough to go over the dining area or up the stairs. Some families who have large Thanksgiving celebrations make the chain in the socializing time before the feast, then it is hung over the table. After the meal, one person (who is good at reading handwriting) can read all the links aloud.

All about YOU. At each place at the table, put a 5" x 7" card and a pen. On the top of the card is written the words: "All about _____." Each person fills in the name of the person on his left, then writes something about that individual for which they are thankful. Next, the card is passed to the right so that the next person can add to the list. When the cards have been all the way around the table, give them to the person as a souvenir of the day. You may also wish to read them aloud.

After the Thanksgiving feast. Sometimes there is a let-down for kids when the turkey is reduced to a carcass and the adults just feel like chatting. One wise mom invented a tradition that has continued many years. She provides paper and marking pens for making pictures about Thanksgiving. For those youngsters who write, she also has a page on which is printed a provocative first line of a story, which each youngster finishes in his own way. The first line might be: "As the Pilgrims and Indians began their feast, a helicopter suddenly appeared overhead" or "The week before Thanksgiving, all the turkeys in the world decided to hold a meeting at Disneyland." When pictures and stories are finished, they are shared amid applause and laughs from the adults.

Neighborhood parade. So everyone has overeaten! One group of neighbors has a healthy tradition for after the feast.

They all parade around the block, chatting with one another, with kids on bikes and babies in strollers—even a few of the older folks in wheelchairs. And one year, when a new neighborhood church had a Thanksgiving evening service, they all paraded to it.

Farewell circle. At the end of the Thanksgiving gathering (or a Christmas or New Year's Eve party), one family has the tradition of a final song, sung in a circle with arms around the shoulders of others. Depending on the occasion, they sing "Auld Lang Syne," "Silent Night," or "Goodnight Ladies." Another family does something similar but holds lighted candles, which they blow out one at a time when the song ends.

Wishbone wishes. When carving a turkey, hang on to the wishbone. Clean it up and hang it up to dry. About a week later, tie a bow on it and have it at the dinner table. Select two family members to pull on the wishbone after they have each thought of *two* wishes. The one who gets the larger piece of the wishbone gets her first wish, the one with the small piece isn't sad because she still gets her second wish.

NEW YEAR'S

Walking potluck. Rather than driving on New Year's Eve, one neighborhood sponsors a yearly "walking potluck." Families go to different houses to enjoy part of the meal and a game. They usually make five stops: for appetizers, salad, casserole, dessert, and finally candy and noisemakers to bring in the new year. The activities include limbo, Frisbee-catching in a large family room, resolution making and sharing, charades, and dancing to recorded music. It's a great and safe tradition for welcoming the new year.

Lunar New Year. Not everyone celebrates a new year at the same time. For many Asians the late winter Lunar New Year is the time for a spirited celebration. One neighborhood group has a traditional party that features ethnic dishes as part of a potluck supper, and both simple and elaborate costumes worn by the participants. From one house with a great view of the city, they can watch a legal fireworks display. It is interesting that as this tradition has grown through the years, the party now includes others whose heritage is Greek, French, Hispanic, and African.

Mythical characters. If it is a tradition at your house to make the tooth fairy, leprechauns, the Easter bunny, Cupid, and Santa Claus part of your family rituals, do a good job of it! Make up fabulous stories about what the tooth fairy does with all those teeth, the naughty tricks of leprechauns, or just how Santa is able to visit the entire world in one night. Then, when the child is ready to set aside the practice of believing in these characters, she can still enjoy the made-up stories and will pass them on to her children one day.

New Year's Day update. Encourage the entire family to contribute items to a "keep drawer" in a desk or cupboard. These could be school papers or pictures, awards and promotions, programs or handouts from events or places visited. By stacking the materials in a drawer, the year's happenings will be in order when you turn the drawer over. Then, while watching the New Year's Day parade and football game on January 1, glue all these items into a scrapbook (if you wish, add photos). Accept help from interested family members! Finally, write explanatory comments on the pages. At day's end, look at the book together, reliving the wonderful year your family experienced together.

Invent a celebration. Don't be limited by the calendar as to when you can celebrate. Make it a family custom to have a party "for no reason at all." Some of these creative parties have included "The Rainy Day Party," at which guests arrived in full and far-fetched rainwear, a party given by folks who were moving and needed help to pack up their house, a sing-along party, and an election day party, at which everyone pretended to be a candidate and was prepared to give a concession speech or a victory speech. At one of the most hilarious spur-of-the-moment parties, the host and hostess (one driving their van and the other driving their car) went to the homes of friends late one Saturday afternoon. They knocked on the door and invited them to immediately "come as you are with what you are doing." There were lots of laughs as the guests climbed aboard carrying such things as the evening paper, a mending basket, a file of bills, a bowl of popcorn—and one man carried his mobile phone. When the scruffy group was assembled at the party-givers' home, it was time for make-your-own pizzas served with a big tossed salad and topped off with pie à la mode. Everyone agreed it was a best-ever party—one that became a tradition.

"Let's do that again!"

Use this space to note your own traditions for holidays.

_____

_____

_____

_____

_____

_____

_____

_____

_____

_____

_____

_____

_____

_____

_____

_____

CHAPTER 10

Potpourri

In collecting traditions for this book, some couldn't be pigeon-holed into one category. So, here's a grab bag of unique ideas for a variety of occasions.

I hope this collection of imaginative traditions will encourage you to take off with new ideas, which will then become your gifts to the future.

First day of school. One grandmother has the tradition of purchasing the outfits for the very first day of school. Every kindergartner wants to look special! For nearby grandchildren, she takes them shopping and guides their selections. For those far away, she purchases the outfit at a chain store that is available in the youngster's area so it can be exchanged if it isn't acceptable. In midsummer she gets the anticipation going by talking about this tradition with the grandchild.

"We don't do windows!" The kids in one family can truly say that, but they DO do drawers, cupboards, and closets! One parent's tradition provides her with freedom from these cleaning tasks. Although her youngsters do get an allowance, they are always eager to earn money for extras. She uses sticky notes to label each area to be cleaned. She marks drawers fifty cents, cupboards (depending on size) are one dollar, and closets are two dollars. Kids put their names on the label indicating they will accomplish the task within a week: emptying, cleaning, and refilling the area. In some cases she indicates that she would like to reload the items herself. And, she gives a ten-cent bonus for items found that were out-of-place or had been lost. She brags that she hasn't done these housecleaning tasks in over a decade.

When someone has died. Sometimes parents err by merely telling a child that someone has died, and saying little more. One family has a tradition that is like a mini-memorial service. They set aside a quiet time to talk about the person who has passed on, sharing the history along with photos, and also recalling good times together. They conclude the conversation with each person telling something they will always remember about the deceased.

Oscar loves you! If you enjoy competition, you'll like this tradition. One family has a yearly competition. It started when the children were preteens, but it continues now via the mail and the telephone. For the Oscar awards, there is always a list of nominees in ballot form printed in the newspaper. This page is copied and sent to the grown-up youngsters and a few close friends, who insist on taking part. Each person chooses the movies, directors, and actors who they think will win. Those who live far away mail in their ballots. Those nearby come to the house for popcorn and view the awards show. Points are given for choosing winners in each category and the person with the highest score gets a prize.

School's out. Children have worked hard during the school year, so the last day of school should be a happy time. One family has a traditional "School's Out" party. They take their children and their children's best friends out to lunch. Other ideas are to have a party at a pool or to go to a movie. Whether school ends at noon or in the afternoon, plan a festive event to mark this achievement.

Travel with the grandparents. Grandparents enjoy giving their grandchildren special times, and these are often the most fun when the time spent is just with one child (two children tend to interact more with each other). To give parents time to be together, one grandmother (she's a saint!) takes a grandchild for a week when the child is two years old. Other travel traditions include taking a five-year-old away for an overnight at some scenic attraction, inviting a twelve-year-old to choose a weeklong trip, gifting high school or college graduates with a longer trip with the grandparents. A couple who live in Hawaii tell how they invite their mainland grandchildren to visit. They say that being together has been most rewarding, especially with the older children. So, as a sixteenth birthday gift, they provide a round-trip ticket to Hawaii and an invitation for a week's stay. And, as the young people have gone on to college and married life, they still remember these precious days with their grandparents.

Teeth cleaning! One family has a tradition that removes the fear of going to the dentist. Parents and children go together to have their teeth cleaned twice yearly by the same dental hygienist. Even though they must wait for one another, it still is an efficient use of time because they only make one trip, and they spend the waiting time reading and playing games. Going as a group makes it more pleasant, and they never forget to make the appointment. On the way home comes the reward: a sugar-free ice-cream cone for each.

Hidden tradition. One woman shares the story of how her mother made her a coat with a fur collar when she was sixteen. She hated the coat because it was not "store bought" and because it did not look like something she would wear. Eventually, after years in closets and hope chests, the coat fell apart—except for the fur collar. Because her sister liked to tease her and was glad that she was never asked to wear it, the woman decided that it would be fun to sneak the collar into her sister's home and hide it somewhere. Although they now live a continent apart, the fur collar always turns up after they've visited each other. One year it was wrapped as a Christmas gift with a note that said it had to be refrigerated and not opened until Christmas morning. The woman admits the collar was once slipped into her mending basket, and, because she doesn't tackle that task often, it was nearly a year before she found it! Crazy traditions like this do add to family fun!

Old shows—new viewers. Parents who fondly remember the family-oriented TV comedies of their youth *(Mr. Ed, Life with Father, Leave It to Beaver, Lassie)* have started a Sunday night tradition: supper in the living room with a video of one of these shows. (These are easily obtained at video stores.) They've noted that there is far more to laugh at during these shows than during current TV "family" comedies (filled with innuendos, infidelity, and insensitivity). At the same time, the old shows portray more wholesome family values.

Mystery messages. When grandparents have finished their visit, they leave behind some surprises for their children and grandchildren. For each person, they write a short note on a 3" x 5" card. Then they hide these in places where they are apt to be found, but not too easily. This tradition provides reminders of the good times they've shared together.

Autumn leaves. One family puts the final leaf raking of

116

the year on the family calendar for a Saturday in early November. It's the custom for each person to ask a friend to help with raking and then stay for lunch. They rake the leaves into piles (with jumping allowed). Then, since fires are permitted, they carefully burn them, enjoying the sweet smell of the leaves. Finally, they sit on the front steps and eat hot dogs and caramel apples as they watch the fires burn out.

Honored person. On the day of the championship game, a big recital or play, graduation, or other important occasion, make it a custom to treat the youngster as a very honored person. This means that others do his chores, he gets to request his favorite foods, and he sits at the head of the table. This is just one of many ways the family can acknowledge good effort.

Saturday fun. If it is a parent's custom to sleep in on Saturday morning, resulting in kids watching mindless television, here's a helpful tradition to upgrade the situation. Saturday morning can include easy-to-eat breakfast snacks with juice containers, a special box of toys and games used only on that day (and changed monthly), and an acceptable video. One family even lays a trail of clues for their grade-schoolers, leading them from bedroom to kitchen to play area.

Hand-me-downs. Among married siblings and cousins who have children, many families have the tradition of handing down clothing from one child to another. While in some instances the recipients loved their new clothes, at other times, it was a less than happy experience. Still, it was the custom to take a picture of a youngster in her cousin's outfit and send it on to the cousin. Now grown, their conversations sometimes include: "Do you remember that scratchy purple sweater, or the bunny pj's we all wore?"

Handy helper. When a grandchild is born, one grandmother goes to care for the baby and help the parents for the first week. Somehow she has the magical knack of getting the baby on a schedule of feeding and sleeping, which makes life easier for the new parents. The grandfather often goes along and runs errands, loads the dishwasher, runs the clothes washer, does repairs, and entertains the older siblings.

Amusing grandchildren. Parents often don't have time for certain activities with their children. One grandparent couple teaches the grandkids all sorts of games, giving gentle lessons in good sportsmanship. They keep a drawer of free prizes from cereal boxes or other giveaways to use as rewards. They also take nature walks to look at insects and their homes, and to inspect moss, acorns, flowers, and water bugs. These activities really help the grandparents to better understand the youngsters while giving them casual time to be together.

Just call. In one family the children having troubles are taught to call on a grandparent to help them. The grandparent can offer possible solutions or pray with the child for an answer. From this early training, many young adults still call their grandparents to talk over challenging situations.

Sayings that last. Most every family has some traditional sayings. It's fun to perpetuate these from generation to generation. These include:
- If you are going to make a speech, get up, speak up, shut up.
- Lack of planning on YOUR part, does not constitute an emergency on MY part.
- If you're smoking in this house, you'd better be on fire.
- If we believe that we can, the job is half done.
- Having bad manners is much worse than being poor.
- The sure way to be disappointed is to always rely on others.
- Goodwill costs nothing, yet it is priceless.
- Some nights the only good things on TV are the vase and the clock.

Playing a play. When children read well, borrow copies of a play from the library. Assign roles among family and friends, and have your own play-reading event. While this activity increases poise and improves speaking ability, it's also much fun. One family has a yearly play-reading party and has occasionally used the mystery play kits available at game stores.

Handprints in cement. Establish this tradition each time you move into a new house. Get a bag of ready-mix cement and prepare it according to instructions. In a suitable place in the patio or yard, make a simple square wood frame. Pour in the cement. Then just before it sets up, let each family member put his handprint in the cement (the dog can make a paw print). Letter initials and date on the square. One family (who never moves) does this each year, and eventually they will have a pathway out to a bench at a view spot.

Joke-a-thon. Add humor to traditional family gatherings by including a joke-a-thon on the agenda. Tell folks in advance that there will be a prize for the funniest story. Help your children practice their joke-telling skills so they can compete.

Look at me! All through the growing-up years have the custom of keeping a bulletin board in a place that is easy for the family to view. By keeping it current, it will be looked at. This communication center can contain the family calendar of activities for the month, home chore lists, photos, important phone numbers, invitations, good schoolwork, and interesting mottoes. Tack a bright red piece of paper on one area of the board and label it "Look at me!" Only place the most urgent messages in this area.

First haircut party. One family creates anticipation—rather than apprehension—when it is time for a child's first professional haircut. The event is talked about many times beforehand. A parent can show that haircutting is painless by clipping off a piece of her own hair. Take along a special envelope to hold a clipping of the toddler's hair, which will later go in the family scrapbook. And do remember to take before and after pictures of the child.

A new home. Get that "new home" feeling the easy way. Sometimes the same things have been in the same places so long, we don't actually see them anymore. A quiet weekend at the end of summer is an ideal time to "repot" your home. For this yearly tradition, choose a day when not much else is going on. Put all the doodads on the dining room table, including any that are stored. Put out-of-place items away and throw away old magazines and other rubbish. Take down all pictures and place them on the floor around the dining room. Rearrange the furniture in the living room, family room, and bedrooms (the last with the help of the occupant). This is a good time to clean carpet spots and dust in distant corners. Then go "shopping" in the dining room and put the pictures in new locations, trying to reuse the same hook locations. Finally, place art objects and other knickknacks in new locations. Put away any leftovers for another time. Sit down and enjoy the new look for your house.

So big! For this yearly tradition you'll need a piece of lumber that is about 1" by 80" (a piece of molding works well). At the same time each year—September 1 or January 1—hold it against a wall and measure the height of each family member. Using a pen, mark the year and the person's name on the wood. Having this measuring pole, rather than using the wall in the family room, lets you take it along if you move. Kids like to see just how much they've grown in a year's time.

Happy farewells. When parents are going out and leaving young children at home, the parting is much easier if you let a child be your personal valet while getting ready. Let them give you advice on choosing jewelry, finding the right shoes, spraying the cologne, selecting what shirt goes with the slacks, and so forth. This is educational and also an occasion for good conversation. One family who has this custom says that the children actually look forward to their parents' going out for a meeting or social event because they find the dressing-up process such fun.

Fire drill. Each year, have the custom of a practice fire drill. Go to each room, especially each bedroom, and talk about alternative ways to get from the room to the outside in case of fire. Indicate an object that could be used to break open a window. Show where smoke alarms and fire extinguishers are and how the extinguishers work. Select an outside place where the family should gather when safely outside. At the same time, talk about what to do in case of other disasters.

A fine serving person. One family never hires outside party help. They have the tradition of training their own youngsters to do age-appropriate tasks: open the front door, take coats, serve appetizers and meals, and even clean up. This leaves the parents free to spend more time with their guests.

No arguments about the past. One family has kept a chart for over thirty years that has settled many arguments about mistaken memories. At the end of each year they fill in the following columns as they pertain to the year: (1) the address and phone number of their home; (2) places of employment for each working family member—and salary; (3) trips taken; (4) other family highlights; (5) important events in the world; (6) pets; and (7) information about each child—birth, grade and teacher, awards, graduation, first job. You'd be surprised how quickly such information is forgotten, and how useful this record will be through the years.

Fifth Sunday. Four times each year, there is a fifth Sunday in the month. One family has the tradition of doing something very unique on this day. They mark the calendar well in advance so every family member can take part. One year they climbed a small mountain together, painted part of an elderly neighbor's house, took a boat ride, and went to two movies with a light supper between them.

Traditional parties. Many families choose special occasions for enjoyable parties and these become part of their family traditions. These include a party on the night of the harvest moon, a Super Bowl party, a party on February 29 every four years, as well as ethnic parties, such as Cinco de Mayo and St. Patrick's Day. Don't wait for a national holiday; start your own traditional events whenever you feel like having a party.

Once-a-year photos. Certain traditions fall in the once-every-year category. Take a picture of each youngster on her birthday, and also get a picture of the decorated birthday cake. When school starts, take a photo of her happily doing her homework. Drape the family over and around your car and take a picture. Each New Year's Day take a picture of the family in front of the house, always standing in the same places and in the same poses.

Yearly meteor shower. Once each year, usually in August, the newspapers give the days and times for viewing the Perseid meteors. Look for a clear night when the moon is new (not visible), and start your own tradition of sitting outside and counting them. Kids enjoy being up in the middle of the night to take part. Using blankets or loungers, face the northeast and you can see from one to dozens of meteors each minute. The display occurs in the sky near the constellation Perseus. Many people make wishes on these "falling stars."

Anniversary album. Start a collection of photos taken on each wedding anniversary. Then, when you reach a memorable date (25th or 50th), combine these into a special album along with pictures of family and homes. Parents can also make retrospective albums to give to their children when they move to their own homes.

Your name is written on the palm of my hand. It was an old middle European custom to write the name of one's beloved on the palm of the hand so it could be seen during the day and the person remembered with love. One family has the tradition of using this phrase "Your name is written on the palm of my hand" as a parting reminder of their love for one another. (You may want to read the passage from Isaiah 49:15-16 that includes: "See, I have inscribed you on the palms of my hands.")

"Let's do that again"

Use this page to record your ideas for great traditions.

_____

_____

_____

_____

_____

_____

_____

_____

_____

_____

_____

_____

_____

_____

_____

_____

_____

The Creation of a Child

When the great Creator makes a child, all the wonders of his creation are components. He starts early in the morning and chooses the hues of dawn for a child's eyes—everything from glowing brown to azure blue. With the crimson of the clouds, he paints the cheeks and then adds the gold of the morning sun or the shimmering darkness of night for the child's halo of hair.

The songs of birds, both warbled and whispered, become the standard for the child's own harp—a voice that is soft and low, as well as bold and strong. God's little lambs who play and skip are

125

the model for a child's happy heart. The quiet animals of his ark are the pattern for a child's own thoughtful times. And the silvery brook's rippling music is like the child's laughter.

From his angels, the Creator gives the child purity and love. And these angels are assigned the jobs of guarding and guiding his beloved child. From his own infinite inspiration, he gives the child the unique abilities and determination to succeed. He then sends this child out to its home, to bring joy to its family.

All God asks is that the parents nourish the child with the same reverence that caused him to create this child as a blessed and essential part of his creation. The schools will educate, the church will inspire, the community will offer opportunities for service to humankind. But wherever the child goes, that child will be God's greatest asset and hope for the future.

So remind your children often that they are the pinnacle of God's precious creation and that wherever they may go, he will care for them with the great tenderness of a loving father and mother.

Truly a child is held in the palm of God's hand.

Index